Finding Horace Pippin

The Story of
The Mary Ann Pyle Bridge Painting

Finding Horace Pippin

The Story of
The Mary Ann Pyle Bridge Painting

by Tom Hughes

ISBN-13: 978-0-578-20913-5

Tom Hughes
www.FindingHoracePippin.com

Printed in the United States of America
First printing August 2018
10 9 8 7 6 5 4 3 2

To Laura my wife and daughters
LF, CM, BP
who always said I should write a book.

ACKNOWLEDGMENTS

I wish to thank my family and many friends who offered help in editing, proof reading and encouragement to continue with this project.

Thank you to Jake for suggesting a plan and keeping me on track, to Opus E Fudd for his persistent fine tuning, to Russell Buckingham for his guidance throughout the entire process of research to final draft, to Jon for his time in examining the painting and to Judith Stein for her amazing book that proved invaluable in my research.

AUTHOR'S NOTE

My story is two-fold. One part is a true story about finding a picture by Horace Pippin and the following 16 months authenticating the painting. In this part names of people are made up to protect their identity except where permission was obtained or where the person is well known as an author.

The second part of my story is a purely fictional account of Horace Pippin's life based on much research and literary license on the author's part.

The story is told in alternating chapters using two font styles to differentiate between the parts. Garamond font is used for the true account of finding the painting and Bookman Old Style font is used for the fictional account of Pippin's life.

Who is H. PiPPiN ?

Years ago, I sold rare books here on Sunday mornings. If you did not arrive by 5-6 am you probably would not snag a space to sell. Today there was only two dealers here. Gino at the bottom of the field and Jim at the top of the field. No sooner did I park when my friend Rickles jumps out of the vehicle to bee line to Jim the book dealer, always trying to nudge me out of finding the first editions. As he went streaming past Gino's booth where I could see an open book next to a painting of some sort. Rickles says, "don't bother it's a fake".

As I pick up the book I notice Gino is watching me from the next table. Even though he is holding a large quilt and explaining its finer qualities to a perspective lady buyer he keeps one attentive eye on me. Gino knows me from many other visits I had made to his tables over the years.

The book is a first edition. It has the same date on the title page as the copyright page. It is an art book of sorts, which does not add much value, unless it is a signed copy by some famous artist such N.C. Wyeth. The book seems to be a catalogue of works by an artist I have never heard of. I put the book down and begin to follow the way Rickles went, who is almost 100 yards away approaching Jim's table, Gino hollers out to me "the painting is 600 dollars". Surprised by the price, I go back and pick up the painting.

It is a landscape scene, oil on canvas board, and the first thing I notice is a ½ inch chip of paint missing near the signature. The artist's signature is the same as the pictures shown in the book. “Hmm interesting” I think as I look for this picture in the catalogue and do not find it. Having never heard of the artist and not having $600, I thank Gino and head towards the parking lot to catch up to Rickles. As I walk along I impulsively pull out my phone and google the name that was on the painting. I am used to this routine now when searching for good books, one of my favorite sites is “AddAll” which scans the world’s book dealers showing the titles and prices of books for sale.

Not having great reception due to a poor cell signal I watch as google search begins to paint results on the screen. I come to an abrupt stop in the empty parking lot as the words National Gallery of Art, Washington D.C. fills in at the top of the search along with the name of the artist that was on the painting I just was holding.

I turned around going into my pockets gathering all the cash I have on me (cash is king at flea markets) and count a total of $290. Seeing me gather the bills in my hand, I now had Gino’s full attention. As I approach, still 30 feet away from Gino, I think I might have a chance at buying this piece of art. Will he take my money, I think to myself?

By now another perspective buyer arrives and picks up the painting. 25 feet, 20 feet, soon the painting will belong to me. Not so easy though, as the man holding the painting shouts over to Gino, “how much for the picture?”

Holding the cash high outstretched in my hand, I still have Gino’s attention. And as I arrive in front of him saying “will you take 290 dollars?”, he grabs the cash out of my hand turning to the other person and declares that the painting is sold. I drain a deep sigh of relief as I thank Gino and head over to retrieve the picture, being that the other man has placed it back on the table and already left. As I fetch my winning piece I once again glance at the book on the table and take note of the title “Works of Horace Pippin, an exhibition at the Brandywine River Museum.”

I put the painting in the back of my vehicle and set off to fetch Rickles, with no intention of telling him I bought it. He would only ridicule me for wasting my money on some lousy piece of fake art work.

Soft Glow.

The yellow glow of the gas lamp magnified the falling snow as young Horace pressed his face against the window pane at the parlor window seat. Would tomorrow be a snow day with school being closed? I hoped so because it was less than 2 weeks until Christmas and I still had plenty of work to do until Santa Claus would come visit. To begin I would have to be sure to be on my best behavior and help Ma whenever I could. Shoveling snow from the front stoop as well as carrying the ashes from the coal stove to the roadside on trash day would be two chores that I could help with today. Ma had said "Bad behavior and you will have coal in your Christmas stocking". There was only 10 more days until Christmas.

The count-down calendar that I started on Thanksgiving after the big feast would need my attention to bring it up to date. Keeping the calendar up to date was most important. It was a drawing of sorts where I had sketched in 30 some boxes on a large sheet of scrap from some package wrappings I saved. Each box was marked with a number starting at 30 and ending with 1 which would represent December 24th, space was left in each box for little notes that I wrote to myself.

About half of the boxes already had notes in them. Such notes included things I was hoping to get for Christmas as well as ideas I had for gifts I wanted to give to my Ma and some friends. For Ma it would be a picture I had made of a reindeer pulling Santa's sleigh over a snow-covered roof with a large sack of packages in his sled.

Since it did not snow enough for school to be closed, the next day dragged on what seemed like an eternity. The bell at last rang and we were dismissed. On the way home from school I found a half used red pencil along the roadside in a small snow bank.

Being Friday I took my time walking along the edge of the paths because this was a trash day. One would never guess what might had fallen to the side when the trash wagons were pulled away. At times it could be messy business with what the horses left behind. Once, there was a doll I found that cleaned up nicely. I gave it to my cousin for her birthday.

With my new found red pencil I could add a bit of color to my drawing. That night I colored the nose of the reindeer in Ma's drawing a bright and shiny red color! And since Christmas was approaching quickly I began crossing off the days with a red X. Soon it was night time and sleep began to overtake me into a wintery dream of streams, woods and covered bridges.

Past Experiences.

Gino was a quick turn over type of dealer. A few years back when I first met Gino on a much busier Sunday, I had a crazy experience. It was early in the morning and I was chatting with a book dealer friend who was considered the best book scout in the region. His name was Opus E Fudd and I had been shadowing him over the years at library sales. I was not stalking him but was just excited to learn about the trade. Opus E Fudd probably pretty much ignored me at the time. He finally accepted my antics and we became friends. By this time in my collecting career I had focused on books. I hardly knew anything about the other treasures one could find at flea markets.

Primitive furniture, all sorts of antiques as well as paintings or pictures were to be had for a price (usually cash). I always thought the term picture meant photographs, "not so one dealer told me, it can mean a painting". Even today I am still learning about this vast world of collectibles.

Today I was to learn an important lesson, "listen to those who know". As I was asking Opus about what books he brought along today he pointed to the two booths down at the end of the pavilion "Do you see that picture hanging there"?

As I turned to look, Opus pushed me in that direction urging me to go buy that painting for 400 dollars. Perplexed I hesitated, only to have Opus firmly tell me "If you do not buy the picture immediately the short stocky man approaching from behind us will certainly purchase it". I had a little over 400 dollars on me, this being my budget for books on this Sunday morning, and I quickly stepped over to the last booth and asked the dealer, who introduced himself as Gino, about the watercolor painting hanging there. Gino said, "400 dollars, that is what I paid at auction this past week and all I want to do is get my money back". I handed Gino $400 in twenty-dollar bills and carried away the winter scene picture of a country church, a watercolor done in a sort of bizarre-like style.

I was already beginning to like this picture. The church windows were allowing the rising full moon to pass its light through them and land softly on the snow-covered road in front of the church. Overall the painting cast an eerie feeling that sort of mesmerized me. The colors were odd dark blues, with blue tinted snow contrasting the deeply rich yellow of the moon. The perspective was off, the trees all pointy with black sharp lines.

Now back at Opus E Fudd's booth with the picture as the other man (years later I would finally meet him) passed us not noticing what had happened with the sale going down. He received me victoriously saying, "good, you got it just in time before the painting collector got there" glancing over to Gino's booth as Amos arrived there. Opus went on to say, "you will not be sorry", as he went to his car to get a large book titled Art Auction Prices. Flipping through the pages leading to the artists whose last names began with "C" he finally settled on one of the entries in this tome of some 500 pages to the name Coopedge, Fern, landscape oil painting, sale price $35,000 dollars. Okay I said, this picture I just brought is signed F. Coopedge it is a water color painting not an oil painting. He looked at me in the eye and said, "do not worry you will do well".

The Pigeon Man.

The next morning as the light of day broke through my small window a pigeon flew off the sill. I arose quickly for it was the weekend with many exciting things to discover. The smell of bacon aroused hunger pains in my belly as I stumbled down the steps pulling up my coveralls. Just outside the kitchen Ma had set out the broom pail and mop for my normal Saturday chores of helping with cleaning the house.

It was not a big job being that the two of us lived in a little 3 story frame building along a side street in a small town. I had my own bedroom on the 3rd floor while Ma had a large bedroom on 2nd floor along with a guest room and one bathroom. My routine was to quickly but thoroughly broom clean the wood floors which covered all the rooms except the kitchen which was finished in linoleum. This being Ma's most important room she insisted on doing the cleaning there herself. Next would be a mop bath for all the areas I had swept starting upstairs and finishing with the parlor, halls and dining room. This being done I was free to do what I wished.

The rising temperature had melted what of left of most snow piles leaving the roads and alleys clear to explore. Leaving the house by the rear yard door I entered the alley behind our house and turned left. This narrow and somewhat hidden path lead past the backs of the other houses on our row which had picket fences and neat gardens laid to rest for the winter. At the end of this alley I crossed the main street on which large single and twin homes were built. Many had expansive front yards, covered porches, bay windows and tall turrets at the upper floors. Having a destination in mind I crossed directly over to the alley on the other side of the road which was large enough to allow horses and carriages access to the rear of the bigger homes.

It was just this past summer that during my

explorations I had meet Mr. Weaver who had just closed the doors to his carriage house back here and was standing there looking up to the eaves of the carriage house.

"Hello young man", he had called out to me with a big smile. This encouraged me to respond, "What a fine day it is today". Introductions exchanged Mr. Weaver said that he knew Ma and had heard some good things about me, especially my skill in artwork. I now remembered that Ma had mentioned a man along here that owned the Inn on Main Street and that she did sewing and laundry for him. Our discussion progressed to all the activity that was going on overhead at the edge of the roof to the carriage house. My Weaver explained that he kept pigeons up there both as a hobby and for sending messages. I would learn that these birds could be trained to go to certain destinations and sent back home with some sort of response. Even though the post delivery was reliable, this method would most of the time be quicker. Mr. Weaver asked if I had ever seen a pigeon coop and would I like to come back soon and visit his?

Excitedly I responded, "I will ask Ma and if it is ok with you I would like to bring along my sketch pad and pencils and make some drawings". We agreed to meet next week on Wednesday after school and I thanked him taking off to return home. As I departed Mr. Weaver called out, "All of the birds have names and you can meet them individually"

Returning home and rushing through the front door, Ma stopped me in my tracks exclaiming, "Horace, why the front door, your boots are still on and you are so excited, did something happen to you I should know about"?

Trying to calm down I stammered, "I met this man, his name is Mr. Weaver, he has birds that carry messages, he said he knows you and that I can go back and meet his pigeons and make drawings"! I went on to tell her about my adventure of meeting the man who owned the Inn and lived in a huge house with a separate building for his carriage and horses which also houses the birds above in the attic. And I told her how he invited to visit next Wednesday after school. Mom said it would be ok if my home work was finished and that I returned before dark.

The Mystery of Paintings.

Over the next two years I would spend hundreds of hours meeting with, talking to and emailing the foremost experts on Fern Coppedge's work. Some would tell me that my water color was not by her. Others would say I cannot tell you she did it and I cannot tell you she did not do it. In other words, they were saying that it may be one of her paintings.

I treated the first possibly valuable painting I purchased the same way I would research a rare book. I study the structure which is the paper, board or canvas it is done on, next the paint or medium used is looked at, then the condition of the painting is noted and finally the content is considered.

This is when the fun begins. The most satisfaction I get out of buying, selling and collecting books is researching the authors and their work. Over the years I have learned a lot of history, lore, writing styles, binding types and printing history of books I found. A systematic approach always helps me in finding results.

So, with the F. Coppedge painting I applied the same methods. In short, I learned that in school she studied art and did mostly water colors (later a wise art dealer explains "the material was cheap, it was what the students could afford"), that she gravitated to a folk art like style where perspective, including lighting was often set skewed in her scenes, that she painted in the countryside outside of Philadelphia and later joined a school known as the Women of 10. She and nine other ladies would travel to Bucks county, 30 miles northeast of Philadelphia to paint landscape scenes. Fern Coppedge's work became more and more popular to the point of commanding the type of prices that were recorded in the book that Opus E Fudd showed me.

I finally sold this water color for $6,000 to a Bucks County collector who already owned dozens of her paintings (mostly oils), he was convinced it was indeed an original picture done by her. I learned some very important lessons that would come in very handy someday. These lessons were to look, listen, act quickly, do not take no for an answer when you think differently, do your research, listen more, stay focused and you will succeed.

Mr. Weaver and his Inn.

"Calm down Horace and slowly explain everything that happened", commanded Ma. "Come to the kitchen, I prepared your favorite lunch", she said as she turned and took off her apron. Over tomato soup and grilled cheese sandwiches we had what I took as my first grown up discussion.

I listened carefully to Ma as she said, "I have known Mr. Weaver for many years now and I do a lot of his sewing and laundry for his Inn, I am glad you have met him, and it is ok to visit him again. He pays me fairly and he is very wise. I encourage you to listen to him. You can learn much from him."

I learned from Ma that Mr. Weaver was a highly regarded gentleman in the community and that his Inn and restaurant were so successful that people came from Philadelphia, Washington and New York to dine there and perhaps stay over. He also keeps a fine garden from which the harvest is enjoyed by the diners at the Inn.

That night in my room I made some pencil sketches of the day's adventures. I first drew a map of the route that I took to Mr. Weaver's carriage house highlighting the alleys and yards along the way and finishing at the building where the pigeons lived. Next, I did my best to draw a picture of the high roof at the top of the carriage house with the hole and landing, where the birds could enter and take off from. I was determined to bring this latter sketch with me on my next visit.

The following Wednesday after school with homework assignments done, I set off for my meeting with Mr. Weaver. Today the sky was overcast and grey and the temperature was almost cold but none of this dampened my enthusiasm to visit and continue my drawings. Retracing my previous steps, now burned in my memory as well in my sketch book, I stopped abruptly at the corner house of the mansion row. It seemed that in was no longer empty, for I noticed movement inside the first-floor windows.

This house, having been vacant for over a year, was one of my favorite places. I could hide under the large porch behind the lattice work invisible to others. I would hear all sort of gossip as neighbors passed by discussing the goings on of the village. Imagine an entire house packed in boxes and delivered by train on flat bed cars. This is exactly what I heard two ladies discussing as they passed by my observation post last Autumn. "Did you see the kit house from Sears Roebuck Company that was left at the train depot yesterday?", one of the ladies asked. Later the local newspaper had reported the entire story about Mr. Fink's new house that came in boxes, almost like a giant set of Lincoln logs. Before the end of the year the house had been assembled on an empty lot on Oak Street and the Fink family was seen moving in their new house before the Holiday season, a record time for building a new home.

The big alley was clear all the way to Mr. Weaver's back yard and I could already see him standing there looking up at the birds. He turned and greeted me by saying, "Not only are you punctual but you are a few minutes early, it is good to see you".

Thank you I replied, "I hope you are well today, I brought along my drawing materials and hope to sketch a view inside the giant birdhouse". We went inside, past the carriage to the ladder type stair at the front of the stable. The horses were to the side in their stalls munching on some sweet-smelling hay. As we neared the top of the floor above I heard the cooing of the pigeons which was very audible and somewhat soothing to the ear. "This is my flock" Mr. Weaver said as he began to name each bird sitting on their perches.

He proceeded to take a small rolled up piece of paper from his pocket and attached it carefully to Godspeed, the pigeon he named after it's flying ability. "This note will be delivered at the grain mill in about 5 minutes and my order for next week will arrive at the Inn before the end of the day". I already had my pencil and pad out and I made a quick sketch of his hands as he released the bird near the open door of the loft. I thought that later I would expand this picture to include some of the features of the entire pigeon coop. I mentally took note of the tins of feed and trays of water neatly arranged about the room and how clean everything was. I could not think of a cozier space for Mr. Weaver's feathered friends to be, sheltered here from the winter cold outside.

Later as we sat together on the steps sipping hot chocolate Mr. Weaver told me how he sent messages to members of the carrier pigeon club, some of which lived as far away as Coatesville about 12 miles from here. This way we could keep in touch discussing the latest news and make plans for future meetings of the club members. He also told me that he knew Ma for many years and that she was very proud of me. "I am thankful to your Mom for all the help she does in keeping the linens so bright and clean for use at the Inn". He mentioned that someday I would have to come to the restaurant for lunch.

I took my departure thanking him for a fine visit and for teaching me many new things and promised that I would share my drawings with him when finished.

The Quest Begins.

Now back at home after dropping Rickles off at his house, I was anxious to have a closer look at my new purchase. It was one of those periods when I was home alone. Most of my family were in China, one daughter studying medicine, another working as a diplomat for the Commerce Department and my wife Laura was also there being the ultimate mom.

I took pictures of the painting, both sides, taking note of a small paint chip missing near the signature at the bottom of the canvas board, the foundation of the painting. I was now able to enjoy the subject of the painting viewing it from different angles and lighting positions. Using simple geometric forms and patterns along with muted colors the artist captured a beautiful country scene depicting snow covered paths that lead to a covered bridge. With some large trees to one side and a colorful sky to the other side.

The picture exhibited a certain winter quietness, it was peaceful and at the same time a certain type of emotion was present, perhaps sadness. Some movement was suggested by the roads or paths flanked by a rural mail box that was open with the characteristic red flag present.

Turning the picture over I noticed that on the back of the somewhat dirty canvas board there was a stamp indicating where the board came from. The picture was framed with a wide and somewhat old pine wood like cornice moldings. I did not much care for the frame thinking it was too bulky for the scene it encompassed.

Wanting to share my find with friends who deal in antiques and art, I took a few pictures and sent off messages and emails and within minutes two of the three contacts got back to me.

Davio who knows artists mostly from the American Modern Era said he doubted it was a real Pippin painting saying he was faked a lot and I would never find one at a flea market.

Russell Buckingham whose phone does not show pictures was excited and asked if he could come see the picture. He himself is an accomplished artist and one who I consider the most knowledgeable on art of all my friends. He was in the area and would like to meet somewhere. We agreed on 30 minutes from that time to meet at a local country store named Boyer's Market.

I found a box a bit larger than the painting, packed it loosely and set out for the market. By now it was mid Sunday morning and Boyer's Market was sort of crowded with the family crowd it draws for breakfast each week about this time. I snagged the corner table out of the bustle and immediately was greeted by my neighbor Joe who asked to join me.

"Please join me", I said, and began to tell him about my find. Joe asked to see the painting and I held it up to the light and he declared that it was cool looking. He also commented that he knows hardly anything about art or paintings.

Entering, Russell spotted us, came over to the table and met Joe. He directly picked up the painting and looking at it carefully gave a very discernable sigh of appreciation.

To me this was a very good sign. "How did you find this? Where was it? Why did I not see it?", he asked, "I am happy for you." As he continued to admire the artwork, Joe said "goodbye", leaving Russell and I to conjure strategies of what to do next.

One needs to understand the habits of "pickers" who frequent flea markets auctions, and antique shows always on the lookout of some treasure or other items to understand what was going on here. In Russell's case he mostly hunts for antiques such as carvings, masks, long swords and many other items that I know nothing about. At the end of such hunts we get together to share our finds and discuss what we might do next with these items.

He suggested I take the painting to an auction house and ask them to sell it, I reminded him of the experience I had in Lambertville NJ concerning the Fern Coppedge painting that I had found a few years ago. Russell agreed that would be a good start and that I should also consider contacting Freemans in Philadelphia and Christies in New York City.

My Pa.

That night as I lay in bed reflecting on today's meeting with Mr. Weaver I thought about my Pa. I had not seen him for over a year now and Ma would always say, "he is with Aunt Sally trying to get better."

I sort of wished he was coming home for Christmas, but Ma had said his condition was getting worse, he was in a big home where he was not allowed to leave. She went on to say, "your Aunt Sally tries to visit him each Sunday".

It was evident Pa was having problems that last day I had seen him, for he once again rushed Ma and myself into the basement during a late summer thunderstorm. He shouted madly about the troops coming again and that finding shelter would be necessary.

This would scare me to death as he huddled us into the coal bin wincing almost to tears. We would usually lose electricity and that would make it darker and more frightening as each crack of lightning and thunder made it seem like bombs exploding around us.

While Pa was in the hospital, Ma told me some of the history. He joined the Union army to go South and fight the Confederates who were trying to overthrow our government. After fighting for a year Pa returned by train along with many other wounded soldiers. He had all his limbs but was greatly shell shocked and prone to constant fits. There were so many injured men at the train station in Philadelphia that it was turned into a hospital to care for them. After many months in bed he returned home for a month or so before he left to be taken care of by Aunt Sally in upstate New York. Ma thought it would be best for Pa to go there because her sister had been a nurse and was now retired.

Is It Real?

Auction houses will occasionally host an appraisal day when one can bring in an article for possible sale and the appropriate department or person would determine a value and sometimes give an opinion on authenticity. However more recently due to lawsuits by buyers who found their purchases to be fake or even sometimes stolen, auction houses have taken a more careful approach.

Having been to the Lambertville Auction House with a painting once before I decided to check their web site for an upcoming appraisal day. I found that there was one scheduled for the following Monday. I wanted to be somewhat better prepared this time. I called Garrett a friend who had considerable experience dealing with this Auction House.

Garrett had been a friend for a couple of years now, having first met him at Adamstown flea market where I brought an old bible from him. He normally doesn't deal in books since they are heavy and hard to sell. About a year ago knowing that I liked books he mentioned to me that he was tidying up an estate sale, that included paintings, furniture and vintage clothing, which are all things that he likes to buy and sell. Also included was an extensive collection of books from the same estate. I went on to purchase about 5000 books from that collection.

I asked him for advice on what to do with the painting. He told me to speak to Tim Smart at the Lambertville Auction House. "He will tell you if it is the real thing. Go on a Monday morning when they have a free appraisal session, and make sure you call Tim in advance and mention my name."

The following Monday morning, having spoken to Mr. Smart on the phone previously, I set off early with my painting and headed to Lambertville NJ. I like driving back roads for two reasons. Usually there is less traffic and I enjoy the landscapes that are along the way. The trip today took me over several covered bridges, but not the one in my painting.

Who Is Santa?

The next morning was exciting because it was Christmas Eve. I wanted to be at my best behavior because Santa (or was it Ma?) would be leaving gifts around the little Christmas tree that we had decorated recently.

I had a plan to solve this mystery about Santa. How could he live in such a cold place called the Artic all year long and how could reindeer fly? I always wondered how could a single sleigh hold enough presents for the millions of homes Santa would visit in one night?

After Ma tucked me in for a good night's sleep I quietly got out of bed and in my stocking feet I slowly descended the front stair to the parlor and quickly hid behind the tall lounging chair. Except for the twinkling lights on the tree it was almost completely dark. I was out of sight here in my hiding place, but I could peek a view of the back of the tree. Ma was in the kitchen preparing for tomorrow's feast and we both were looking forward to Aunt Sally's visit. Ma's sister was expected to arrive on the first train in the morning.

Startled, after dozing off I wondered why I was propped up against the big chair in the parlor. Ma's soft footsteps brought me back to my secret mission of finding if Santa was real. Ma continued to set wrapped presents around the tree. A large one with a red bow had my name on it. When she finished Ma turned the tree lights off and quietly made her way up to bed.

Waiting twenty minutes or so and not hearing any noise upstairs I returned to my bedroom and settling in I victoriously sighed, "Mystery solved, Ma is Santa Claus".

Aunt Sally arrived early, for I was awakened by spirited laughter from the kitchen below. Both were catching up with the latest family news.

I quickly dressed and ran down the back stairs to the kitchen, as I cried out "Merry Christmas". Aunt Sally spread her arms wide as I literally flung myself into them almost toppling the chair. She had not seen me since last Easter and was amazed by how I tall I had grown! She exclaimed "My how you have sprung up young man".

Aunt Sally was my favorite relative and since she lived close to where Pa was, I hoped she had some good news about him. Having anticipated my question, she diverted my attention by saying, "There are many unopened presents around the tree in the parlor including a large box with your name on it". As I headed in that direction I surprised both ladies by claiming, "I know all about the Santa Claus thing".

Having a plan in mind I opened all the small presents first, next looked in my stocking hanging by the fireplace, no coal in there, and finally tore open the big box. Hours must had passed for I heard Ma and Aunt Sally still talking quietly in the kitchen while the great aroma of a turkey roasting wafted this way.

The present in the big box had occupied all my attention. I had already assembled the wooden easel, set up the large sketch pad and was in the process of drawing a panoramic view of all things about Christmas that I could see in the parlor. This sketch I would give to Aunt Sally before she returned home.

It seemed that Ma aka Santa had finally realized that I was so keen on becoming an artist.

Do the Homework.

Lambertville is a small town on the eastern side of the Delaware River, about half way between Easton to the north and Doylestown to the south.

A decent size crowd of antique dealers, collectors and enthusiasts like myself assembled inside a large gallery in the building. I spotted Tim Smart immediately, he was just a few years older than myself. He signaled to me to come over, seeing that I had the painting.

After pleasantries were exchanged he carefully examined both sides of the picture. While admiring the context of the work he said "right age, right style. I would like my painting expert to look at it, so take a seat over there and she will be out shortly".

It was not long until a younger lady carrying a laptop sat down across from us asking "who is first"? Although I had been there longer than the person next to me, I offered that she go ahead of me and she did, also carrying a painting to the desk. Another 20 minutes or so passed, it was my turn.

With much interest Jane, the painting expert, looked over my picture. Going from computer to canvas I believe she was comparing it to the other works by Pippin displayed from the internet, she repeated what Mr. Smart said, "right age and right style!"

Looking up to me, "you really have to do some homework with this and somehow have it authenticated". Seeing my puzzled look Jane explained that Horace Pippin, although somewhat famous had not produced a whole lot of work and that most of what he did was catalogued from shows in the past. Once certified as a real Pippin, she told me that they would be interested in putting it up for auction if I decided to sell it.

Well, somewhat perplexed I asked Jane for some advice on what to do next as far as the "homework" both she and Tim said was necessary. To my surprise she said to start at the Philadelphia Library. "There you will find copies of catalogues of many shows that featured Pippin's work". I thanked her, said good bye to Mr. Smart, packed up my painting and headed back home.

Bad News about Pa.

The discussion in the next room had become serious. Ma and her sister were whispering. Wandering into the kitchen I asked, "How is Pa"? Aunt Sally told me that his condition had worsened, and that Ma and I should consider moving to her house to be closer to Pa. This would require me changing schools and even though children were not allowed to visit the home he was in, Ma would be able to see him more regularly.

So it was decided that Ma and I would return with Aunt Sally to upstate New York and move in with her for the remainder of my school year. Being half way through sixth grade, this would be a challenge for me.

On Friday of the following week all three of us boarded the train that would stop in New York City and then go on to Aunt Sally's home town. We had packed four large trunks and I was able to fit all my art materials including my Christmas present.

I was surprised but very happy Mr. Weaver showed up to see us off. He handed Ma an envelope and said, "please encourage Horace to keep up drawing, he has a lot of talent". For Christmas I had giving Mr. Weaver my completed picture of the birds and pigeon coop, he loved it, saying, "I will frame this and hang it in my den". I had thought very good about this for it was the first picture of mine that someone other than family would be displaying.

Feeling much more like a young man as the train pulled out of the station, I wondered what lay ahead. We were leaving behind the house I grew up in and even though Mr. Weaver, the Inn owner we rented from had said do not worry, I had some concerns, not knowing what the new year had in store for us.

Doubts in the Studio.

Driving home from Lambertville it occurred to me I would be passing by the home of Amos, a painting consultant who I know by appearance but never met in person. My wife had met Amos, and both Rickles and Russell knew Amos well. "He is the go to person to have paintings restored", Rickles always said.

Being an artist Russell had said "be careful who you ask to fix a picture, there is a lot involved from paint material to foundation, brush strokes and many other factors that need to be considered when a painting is cleaned and restored". Taking this to heart I still decided to visit Amos, not to enlist his help with restoration, but just to show him my picture and get his opinion on its authenticity. I also wanted to see his house, I was told it was a rustic type cabin that was sitting on the edge of the woods.

I contacted him on the cell phone and got his address. He warned me that cell reception was bad at his place and I may have trouble finding it. Google maps indicated that I was about thirty minutes away.

It was a good thing I had taken a screen shot of his place on Google maps before I departed because fifteen minutes later my cell phone had no signal and oddly enough Google maps stopped returning a location, which very seldom happens no matter where I travel.

Another 20 minutes after climbing and descending through remote ridges I spotted Amos on the roadside, he was waving to me having recognized my approaching van. He directed me to turn into a rocky maintained drive. About 15 feet or so to the right was a small log home. The view from here back across the road was stunning!

Russell had mentioned there also was a separate studio building where Amos did restoration of paintings as well as creating his own art. I said, "what an amazing homestead, is this also your studio?" Pointing up into the woods he replied, "It is under construction, although I do some work there, most of my projects are currently in the log home."

We proceeded to the porch of the cabin. Inside was a great room with a galley kitchen to one side and a small wooden table and antique wood stove on the opposite side. Windows from the front porch and rear lit up an old landscape painting he was restoring. Behind were additional pictures including some of his original art work. There was a ships ladder in the corner of the room reaching up to what I assumed were the sleeping quarters.

I asked him how he found this place. Smiling he replied, "My wife and I moved here a year ago after I made a trade with a client who exchanged the property for having me restore some art work for him". He asked if I brought along the painting. Pointing to his laptop on the table he said, "I brought up some images of Horace Pippin's work, I don't think your painting is one of his". Going to my van to fetch the painting I thought his statement a bit strange since he had not seen it yet.

I carefully removed the picture from the box. He took it by the edges of the wide wooden frame examining the back first. "cardboard/canvas board about 1 ½ x 2 feet in size, never removed from this frame," he observed out loud. Turning the picture over and holding it up to the window for better lighting Amos went on to say, "needs a bit of repair and it is signed H. Pippin, however I am sorry to say that this is not one of his works".

Startled, I asked, "how can you tell so quickly?" I can give you three reasons he said, "it has never been taken out of this frame which is not old enough to be from Pippin's time, secondly, if you compare it to his paintings there on my computer you can see that it does not come close to any of them in appearance and finally, I doubt a Pippin would be at a flea market in Adamstown!"

I thought to myself that if this was an old book I would retort with several reasons why I believed it could be the real thing. However, not knowing much about paintings to begin with and knowing less about Horace Pippin except that he was from West Chester, PA and died young and that he painted most of his work in the 1930s and 40s I decided to remain quiet. Probably looking a bit disappointed and taking the painting back from Amos I said, "thank you for looking at it, I really enjoyed visiting and seeing your place here, best of luck with the rest of the restoration of the buildings".

Waving from the departing van I was resolved to discuss with Russell what had happened here at Amos's place and ask him if I had made a mistake in buying the picture in the first place. My thoughts now were, I paid 290 dollars for this, I like covered bridges, I really enjoy this picture and it would look nice displayed in my library at home.

Settling In.

Aunt Sally made us feel at home especially on New Year's Eve. She knew from Ma how I loved to make pizza from a box. So, on the last evening of the year we set about cooking in Aunt Sally's kitchen.

It always amazed me how the little box of ingredients that included a package of yeast, a can of tomato sauce with lots of oregano, a bag of flour and a container of grated cheese could all come together as my favorite food treat. It was magic to me to see the yeast bubbling in warm water before adding the flour to produce a stretchable dough that would rise in a warm place. I even taught Aunt Sally the trick of turning the dough over the corners of the flat rectangular pan so that if would not spring back towards the center. Once in the oven all the flavors began to mix into the most amazing aroma I can think of. Later as an adult I would still remember this special event whenever I pass a pizza stand at the local carnival.

The winter passed quickly and uneventful except for a letter I received from Mr. Weaver relaying a story about young Abe Lincoln. He had chopped down a cherry tree against his father's wishes but told the truth when asked if he was the person who did it. This story inspired me to create a picture depicting this scene. After working on it for about 5 weeks coloring it with some dark pencils and using the red one for the cherries, I was pleased with the results. This would be Ma's birthday present this coming May.

The Quest Continues.

The next day I met Russell for breakfast and shared my experience with Amos. "I am very surprised", he said, "I've known him for many years and this is one time I totally disagree with him. His comments hold no bearing because they are not directly relevant to the painting."

He went on to say that the frame statement does not apply because I know frames and it could be from the late 30s or 40s. You should talk to a professional framer and have that confirmed. Also, Amos is not an expert on Pippin, so he would not be familiar with his works and I wonder if he ever saw one in person. And finally, items of high value are often found at flea markets such as Adamstown.

He mentioned a painting his friend bought there last year for 500 dollars only later to sell it for $60,000. He also researched auction sales finding that a Pippin painting sold at auction in Philadelphia over 30 years ago for $123,000 dollars.

Russell is a very accomplished artist, I value his knowledge of antiques and his ability to spot quality artwork. As much as I want my find to be the real thing, if Russell thought the picture was a fake, he would tell me, and I would honor his opinion.

Although Russell again suggested I approach some other auction houses and sell the painting, I decided it was time to do some serious investigation of Horace Pippin and his paintings. I would start at the Philadelphia Library as suggested to me and by researching frames on the internet.

A Very Bad Summer.

The summer passed by quickly and I was glad. It was the worst period I could remember. Ma had trouble finding work and Pa's condition continued to worsen. I managed to catch a glimpse of him from afar when Ma and Aunt Sally took me along to the home he was admitted to. Although only adults could visit I saw Pa from a distance, slumped over on a lawn chair with the ladies at his side pointing to me behind the fence.

He never looked my way which told me he was bad off. A week later Pa passed away and we buried him in the local cemetery. It was a very strange thing burying Pa, I had never known him very well and I did not feel any grief until many years later when I would experience some of the same horrors of war that he had been through.

Vintage Frames.

That night searching eBay for vintage wooden frames, I found several wide pine frames with similar profiles to the one used with my Pippin painting. Most were listed as being from the late 1930s to the mid-1940s.

The next day I visited the local arts tore in Kutztown early in the morning knowing that they were open for only half a day. At the front counter I asked Milton if Katrina was there? He replied, "do you have a drawing you would like to have mounted?"

Over the years I had learned of Milton's appreciation of fine books always sharing with him my better finds. I would ask him for suggestions on art materials that I could use for the book boxes I would make for my finer books.

Milton went on to ask, "what interesting book have you discovered lately?" I said, "not a book but a painting," and I began to show him pictures of the covered bridge painting. After commenting on how beautifully the picture was he went on to ask if I wanted to see Katrina about reframing it.

I wanted to ask how old she thought the frame might be. "It looks vintage era to me", Milton said pointing to the rear door, "she is out back in the frame shop." Although I had spoken to Katrina many times, but I never really had introduced myself properly, so I greeted her at the door telling her my name and why I had come. "I remember seeing you here many times over the years" she said.

After some short talk she asked to see the pictures of the painting and frame. "I really love the painting, some beautiful colors hiding there under the surface." She went on to tell me that she had been framing here for 35 years and at another gallery for 10 years prior to this job. "I can tell you that the frame around the covered bridge picture could easily be from the early 40s or before". "I handled many old wide pine frames like this in my experiences." She asked what I intended to do with the painting.

I shared my limited knowledge of Horace Pippin and told her that I was on a quest to it have it authenticated. Thanking her I headed out, and she wished me luck with my project.

Big Changes.

It became more difficult staying at Aunt Sally's place, Ma could not find work being in a new area, not knowing anyone. I decided to drop out of school, so I could help bring in some money. I was able to find part time work as a delivery boy and learned how to pack artwork for a dealer who would ship pictures across the country.

There was not much time to draw and I missed it greatly. But I always carried a pocket sketch pad where I could record a quick scene that might catch my eye. That winter as I was taking a walk down a snow-covered path I saw a red fox run ahead of me and recorded it in my note book. There was something very moving and at the same time a peaceful pattern arose from the even rhythm of the animal's tracks in the freshly fallen snow. Latter I would turn this sketch into a major painting I would create, exhibit and sell to a collector of art.

Time seemed to fly by after Pa's passing and before long I was facing a major decision of leaving Ma and joining the army to help fight with the allies in Europe. The benefits of joining up were attractive. I would be following in Pa's footsteps, I would also be able to send my pay back home to help Ma and Aunt Sally cope with ever growing expenses.

So as a young man I joined the all black infantry out of Harlem in NYC and went off to training camp. After a brief period learning the basics of surviving in trench warfare I boarded a huge ship and headed overseas to the front in France with 2000 troops on board to fight against the Germans.

Tracking the Picture.

Three Sundays after buying the Pippin painting I decided to visit Gino at the flea market to ask him where he acquired it. It was a cold damp day, I set out early knowing Gino never misses a day setting up no matter how bad the weather is. I was alone this time deciding not to ask Rickles to join me.

Again, Gino was one of only a few dealers there and I wondered how much longer it would be until he would relocate up the road to the larger market. This is probably the reason the Pippin painting was not snatched up by someone else three weeks ago when I found it.

Gene recognized me as I approached and nodded when I said good morning. I asked him. "where did you find the painting, I bought from you a few weeks back?" Remembering me, he said got it at auction in the Lancaster area the Tuesday before in a box lot of items, paid a few hundred dollars for it and I bet that it is worth at least ten thousand dollars or more."

Not wanting to pursue a discussion since he is very difficult to talk to most times, I thanked him and left after taking a glance at the items on his tables. No paintings there today. In the past 4 years I saw only three pictures he had for sale.

That night I did some research on auction houses in the Lancaster area and found one that held weekly auctions on Tuesdays. Accepting items from the Wednesday before for their photo preview section of their website. However, they also took in items right up to the beginning of the Tuesday sale, this included box lots. I researched the preview pictures for the auction and found no picture of my painting. So, it probably came in later and was not photographed.

This all made sense to me reinforcing Russell's statement that valuable and collectable items can always slip through these sales

Satisfied I went to bed determined to visit the Philadelphia Library the next morning to follow up on the lead that the expert at the Lambertville Auction House had offered.

Life in the Trenches.

The stormy nights in the basement with Pa screaming about shells and bombs did little to prepare me for the real warfare that raged about me for the next year.

My pocket diary sketch book was my only solace. I recorded mayhem in the trenches by observing the action and drawing a record of it for later use. Some of these scenes include a German plane on fire crashing to the ground after being hit by gunfire from one our planes. Another is a picture of us running up a hill as cannon shells burst all around us. Often in the trenches we wore our masks to protect us from German gas, so I made a sketch of this.

For many winter weeks the trenches would shake from exploding shells all around us. It was the extreme cold and frost that held the earth together and prevented it from crumbling and burying us alive. Towards Spring with warmer weather, the Germans began an onslaught with tanks, machine guns and soldiers with rifles and bayonets, they came at us horde after horde.

I did not understand that by holding this endless linear pit meant we were winning, but the attacks lessened and finally stopped all together. However, our loss of soldiers was great with only about a quarter of us remaining. Most of us had bad injuries including burns, loss of hearing and some even lost an arm or hand.

After receiving an all clear message we came out of the trenches and began a long march across the devastated landscape towards a village to be picked up and transported to the coast. On the second day of walking I took a sniper's bullet in my right sketching arm. I was badly wounded but my pleas against amputation won and I was patched up as best could be.

I fought off infection for the next few weeks and was finally at the port waiting for a ship back home. By now news of the war ending was all around and there were great celebrations everywhere.

Our regiment was now named the Harlem Hellfighters and we received special commendation from the French President. Another long ocean trip lay ahead. It passed quickly as I was heavily sedated to help reduce the pain from my injury.

Library Research.

Sitting with the Director of Art Books at the Philadelphia Library, I was thinking why I had I never heard of Horace Pippin before this.

After all, my sister was an artist, I often visited art museums, I enjoyed reading about art and artists and I occasionally did buy some pictures when they appealed to me. The Director whose name was Anna explained to me that Horace Pippin was somewhat unknown in the general art world but was a major player in American Folk Art and Outsider Art circles.

She said he died young not having produced many works. But this does not diminish his stellar run as a local artist who went on to become nationally acclaimed very quickly.

His pictures hang in many of the major museums around the country with several here in Philadelphia. You can see his work at the Philadelphia Museum of Art, the Barnes Foundation and the Pennsylvania Academy of Fine Arts all within a five-minute walk from here.

Thanking her I asked, "would there be materials that I could research to learn about Horace Pippin showing her a picture of the painting. "That is a very nice picture," Anna said, continuing "we are currently displaying a catalog of Pippin shows over the years in our entrance showcase". She went on to explain they are from our archives and not often shown, you can view them from outside the glass doors, however they will not be available for close examination until next month.

I can show you several books on Pippin from our stacks. Suggesting that I go to the lobby and view the display case while she retrieved the books, I headed that way.

I found the display of catalogues at the top of the main steps in front of a large well-lit reading room. However, from outside the locked case not much discernable. I could see that the catalogs were rather small pamphlets dated from the late 30s and early 40s each about 10 pages or so. They seem rather delicate, perhaps from their age, but I already planned that I would return in a few weeks to examine them closely.

Returning, I could see that there was a neat stack of volumes on the desk in front of Anna. Across was an empty table and chair so I moved the pile of books to have a look.

There were three volumes that I was most interested in, a copy of the exhibit book that was on the table when I bought the Pippin painting and two retrospectives of Pippin and his work. One of these was titled "I Tell My Heart" by Judith Stein and it seemed to be the most informative, so I asked if I could borrow it from the library. Anna said "sure, just check it out downstairs in circulation and don't forget to stop back in a few weeks to examine the catalogs and pamphlets more closely."

Ma is Gone.

Sadly, back home I found Aunt Sally alone to greet me at the dock. She was in black and I knew then that Ma would not be coming. She had died of the flu weeks earlier and there was no way for me to know this. Holding each other in a strong embrace Aunt Sally said, "you will come back and live with me Horace".

Settling in with Aunt Sally was not easy. I still had little use of my injured arm, I was missing Ma and I found it almost impossible to return to my art work. I did however find work at a local gallery and help pack and ship items that had sold. I also started to find junk and resell it on tables I would set up near the local market. Once I found a post card that reminded me of a small village in France that I had passed through on my way home. It inspired me to try again to do pictures.

Aunt Sally had suggested that I use my good left hand to guide my injured arm and see if I might be able to sketch a few things. After many weeks of painful attempts, I managed to at least make some designs in wooden boards using a burning tool. Practicing this technique, I began to add colors to the carved like drawings and was pleased with the results. I showed myself that I could still create art work.

On a delivery to a laundry shop I met a lady working there who caught my eye. Her name Jannette and she seemed interested in meeting me. We started going out and before long were engaged to be married. Aunt Sally liked her, commenting she reminded her of her late sister.

Jannette and I married that summer and with my small pension, odd side jobs and her work as a freelance seamstress we decided we could afford our own place and made plans to move back home to West Chester. I had written Mr. Weaver and found that our old rowhome was still empty and available for rent or purchase. Mr. Weaver read about the

Harlem Hellfighters and said he was proud of my courage in defending the nation.

I Tell My Heart.

At home that night I began to read Judith Stein's book," I Tell My Heart". She had met Horace Pippin, probably at Pennsylvania Academy of Fine Arts (PAFA) where he was an adjunct teacher at times. Judith also taught there and later had organized a major show of his work.

In "I Tell My Heart" which is a definitive research guide on Horace Pippin's paintings, Judith brings the reader very close to his art. So close that I felt I knew him. In my opinion Judith was an expert on Pippin. I found that she was still alive and living in the Philadelphia area, but I had no contact info on her.

So, I began to search for cross references between her and Pippin's art. One result concerned an art critic circle that she served on many years ago hosted by a still active art scholar. An email to him explaining my Pippin painting and the research I was involved in trying to have it authenticated was promptly answered. I will forward your inquiry and questions to Judith for I am still in touch with her.

While I waited for a response from Judith, I continued to study her book comparing my painting to the many examples contained in it. It was like having a forensic expert by my side. No detail went untouched concerning his art.

About 10 days or so passed and I finally received a response from Judith through the art critic. It was a bit disappointing because she seemed to skirt over the fact that I had found a Pippin picture and instead referred me to another person who was working at the Metropolitan Museum of Art in New York City and who was writing a book about Horace Pippin.

Well I thought to myself at least this was not a dead end. Thinking that Judith may not be as active in art circles these days, it was her book that was offering the best info on Pippin.

I followed her advice and sent an email to the Met person, this time including two photos of the covered bridge painting, front and back images. Later I was to regret having done so, I had no idea at the time why.

A Fine Welcome.

When we arrived back home I was not prepared for the reception that met us there. It was truly moving to see Mr. Weaver on the train platform leading a small parade of town folk. Out front with him was the local VFW band and several uniformed soldiers carrying flags and banners.

Holding Jannette tightly by my side I did everything to hold back tears. After the hardships of war, losing Ma and returning with a very bad arm, here I was safe at home. I looked forward to returning to my art studio to tell the stories I remembered.

We worked out a deal with Mr. Weaver to buy the same house that Ma and I had lived in. Jannette was asked to help with his Inn's laundry and seamstress jobs just as Ma had done. The Inn and restaurant had expanding with a new wing being added on for the increase in business.

Finding work was a bit more difficult for me with the use of only one arm, however I managed to find odd jobs around town. Coupled with my volunteer activities with the Boy Scouts and the VFW, I was quite busy during the daytime. And with warmer weather coming I started my plants in the cold frame out back. This year I would also try to keep bees. They would be beneficial for the plants and fruit trees. I found a sting or two from them would help my injured arm feel better.

All this activity left little time for my drawings, so I would stay up half the night with a light burning in my 3rd floor studio. Sometimes the neighbors would comment on how I could survive without any sleep.

One day after repairing a chair in the restaurant at the Inn, Mr. Weaver invited me to his table in the corner to join him for a beverage. Here he explained how he had read a newspaper account of the return from the war of my Regiment in Harlem, New York. He thanked me for my service to our country and wondered how we were able to prevail under such challenging conditions.

Taking out my sketch book dairy, it still amazed me that it survived the long trip home with me, I told him that being able to draw the stories of my experiences helped me to go on.

Mr. Weaver suggested turning the sketches into paintings so that the stories could be shared with others.

Taking his encouragement, using the burning tool, I began making my first picture that night. I traced out the outline of characters and other parts of a scene that would represent my return home from the war. Some left-over house paint that I salvaged recently would be used to fill in the areas that were outlined on the wood board.

The Making of a Pippin Picture.

While waiting for a reply from Judith Stein's referral I continued to learn much more from her book. Of all the pictures in the book there was no mention of a covered bridge painting.

What I did learn was that Pippin often painted on canvas boards, which was the foundation for my painting. Being of very modest means and given that art materials were expensive, Pippin would use whatever paints he could get his hands on. He often used the remains of house paint he found in discarded cans. His paintings were of base and muted colors such as, white, yellow, blue, black and green, all popular house paints in those days.

Judith describes the style of Pippin's pictures consisting of flat forms, unusual color combinations and not much perspective was used. Geometric shapes and forms were widely used. These characteristics were evident in the Mary Ann Pyle Bridge painting.

Pippin would often layer assorted colors to create totally new hues as Stein calls out in the portrait of the Deputy Sheriff. The same effect is evident in Saturday Night Bath at the center top part of the rear wall. The sky in the Mary Ann Bridge picture is also of the same nature. The same layering effect is evident at the edges and rear of the canvas boards that Pippin used, as Stein illustrates in The Getaway painting by Pippin. She says, "Also evident on the reverse (rear or back of the support) are brighter blue colors in the sky than are now visible on the front and red under layers to what are yellow-gray clouds". This same condition occurs on the rear of the board in my painting directly behind where the sky is on the front of the board.

Dorothy Miller quotes Pippin as noted in Stein's book, "How I Paint; The colors are simple such as brown, amber, yellow, black, white and green", these are the colors used in the painting of the Mary Ann Pyle Bridge.

Horace Pippin often added a splash of red color to his scenes which I learned from another book I researched titled "A Splash of Red" by Jane Bryant. She writes that Pippin mostly used somber colors of war such as gray, black and white, however here and there he would add a splash of red. In the covered bridge picture, a splash of red occurs as the flag on the mailbox.

Lost in the Wood Going Home Picture.

I would name my first painting, "Lost in the Wood Going Home", being that I used a wood board and I depict my way home from the war lost in a wood that shows the destruction all around us during the war. The snow shows a slow progress of being lost and the repeating pattern of foot prints emphasize the long way to home.

It takes me a long time to complete this picture. When I am finished I realize I can use my good arm well enough to guide my bad one to continue telling my stories with my pictures. The next picture will be a project that takes three years to complete. There will be other pictures done in between but this current one is complex.

I wish to tell the story of all the equipment, arms and other things I encountered during the war on the frame and continue the story on the canvas depicting a powerful event, as the Germans are surrendering. This work took so long because I kept adding layers and layers of paint coming to terms with my memories. It has a sculptural effect along the frame symbolizing the seemingly endless time and space we were restricted to.

The so-called war series pictures continue with my next few paintings such as Gas Alarm Outpost and Dog Fight over the Trenches.

Question Mark.

I finally heard back from the scholar who sadly says that she found my painting nice and interesting but doubted that it was done by Horace Pippin. She gave two reasons both surprising me, "the signature on your painting is out of scale to the size of letters Pippin used on his other paintings and the canvas board of your painting comes from Pittsburg as the stamp on the back indicates, so this could not have been done by Pippin". There was no mention of the many similar characteristics depicted Judith Stein's book that show up in my covered bridge painting. Later I am to find out this same person did some of the research for Judith's book, which would further puzzle me.

Soon I would meet someone who will tell me the world of buying and selling art can be tricky, dirty and sometimes scandalous. Two groups of people will offer opinions on my Pippin picture, "those who would pooh-pooh my find because it was not their picture and those who would be supporters because of their objective experiences and understanding of fine art."

The scholar mentioned sharing my emailed images of the covered bridge to a friend at the Met who was very knowledgeable with folk art and Pippins work. I replied, "thank you for your time and please let me know if you hear anything from your friend".

Another week passed with no progress in the authentication process. A few trusted friends said my picture was a Pippin. Several others, including an expert said, "no not done by him". I became resolved to approach this project in a serious manner. I would begin to invest a lot more time in research and begin to write an objective report showing it was the real thing.

My Art Becomes My Life.

Painting became the focus of my life. Since art supplies were expensive, beyond my means, I found ways to supply my studio. Jannette and I hardly made enough money for our daily living needs, so I had to be inventive and lucky in finding materials. I would search sidewalks and alleys on trash days looking for near empty paint cans, brushes and wood for frames.

One day while visiting Mr. Weaver I noticed some men doing a major repainting of his expansive house. I asked what happened to the empty paint cans and was rewarded with an offer of them being set aside for me. This was like winning a raffle, for there was enough residue paint to last me awhile.

This common house paint was not of the same quality as the little tubes of oil colors for sale at the art store. However, it offered me a way of obtaining much needed supplies for my studio. It limited my palette to basic colors of green, grey, black, brown and white, all popular colors for houses in this area.

Canvas boards were also expensive but still cheaper than the expensive canvases and stretchers that were commonly used for oil paintings. I made effective use of the boards by cutting the larger more common size boards down to several smaller sizes.

Revisiting my diary from the war and my sketch books from my childhood days I worked passionately every night to produce pictures that told the stories coming from my heart.

Good Advice to Come.

One day in Philadelphia talking to a client the discussion turned to my painting. Jake was an artist and had asked for ideas on converting one of his galleries. He was intrigued with my evolving story about my Pippin picture and suggested I show it to him. He would offer advice on how to proceed with my project. We agreed to have dinner the following Wednesday. I thought it would be well worth the investment it would cost me for a delicious meal for two.

In the meantime, I contacted my friend Mike who collected outsider art. When he studied the photos, I sent him he responded, "you did not tell me it was signed!"

He suggested I contact a friend of his who was a major collector to ask for advice. That person told me to call Jon Harvard at a gallery in Philadelphia and inquire about an appraiser who might be helpful in obtaining an authentication. Making a note of this I looked for some appraisers on the internet.

Making Ends Meet.

Between odd jobs about town during the daytime and painting late into the night in the upstairs bedroom turned studio I began in earnest to pursue what I loved most, a career in creating art.

The only problem was finding a way to financially support ourselves with pictures. Jannette and I hardly managed to scrape by with my meager wartime pension, odd job income and her small earnings doing laundry and seamstress work.

I began to trade some of my pictures for goods and services. I gave a painting to my barber in exchange for a haircut. The barber had seen me one day making a small colored sketch of birds on the fence alongside his shop. "My, what a folksy little drawing you are creating there, is it for sale?", he had exclaimed.

A new pair of work boots came my way from the shoe store owner who liked a picture I displayed there for a while. These successful trades helped me gain confidence in my work as well as providing a much-needed supplement to our daily livelihood.

Becoming Focused.

On Tuesday I spent a good part of the day researching the signature and canvas board questions raised by the scholar. I closely studied the size of the way Pippin would sign his paintings by looking at 20 examples. The style of his signature varied a little but the format he used was consistent.

Judith Stein states in her book that Pippin usually signed his work with a capital H and capital P's and N's, with lower case i's. This lettering style also matched Pippin's signature in the painting I had.

The company stamp on the back of the canvas board read A.B smith Co., Pittsburg and gave an address. An internet search showed that they were in business from the early 1900s and still thrived today. An email was answered with a positive response from the grandson of the company founder, stating that they distributed their art supplies widely during the time my painting was done. It was very likely bought in or near West Chester.

I was beginning to gather some sound objective information that would help me form the basis of the report I planned to complete to help authenticate my picture as one done by Pippin.

Good Things Begin to Happen.

Working late on my pictures, I became somewhat of an icon to the locals who would comment, "When do you sleep? Mr. Pippin, for we see you in the window of the top floor at your easel well into the midnight hours!"

They were correct, for I was getting very little sleep these days after being encouraged by the local shoe store owner who told me he was enjoying my picture so much that I should consider hanging some of my other works in his shop window for sale. If I were to do this and the pictures sold I would need additional ones as replacements.

So I set about working long hours into each night and began to produce more paintings. Two of the newer ones were hung in the shoe store window and I watched in fascination some days as people would stop and stay awhile studying my work. A reporter for the local newspaper was one observer. He called on me one day and asked to do an article in the paper with a photo of one of my paintings. I was thrilled and agreed, asking him to take a picture of the painting I just finished depicting the brick houses along the street on which I lived.

More Discoveries.

On Wednesday morning I received a reply from one of the appraisers I contacted stating that they would be glad to look at the painting. Encouraged by this latest development, I made a mental note to call them the next day.

I arrived at Jake's gallery at that evening with the painting wrapped up in a box under my arm. He greeted me asking, "is that the picture"? I shook hands and replied yes.

Crossing the gallery to a table I carefully took out the painting. There were a couple of more tiny paint chips peeling off near the signature and I was worried it would spread and affect the letters.

He commented on how nice the picture was, how it was beautifully composed and painted. Turning the board over he mentioned it was exhibited in the past. He pointed out clean outline of where a rectangular exhibitor tag had been as paste was applied. And next to it another ghost mark where it had been stuck in place.

I thought to myself how many other details about this piece of artwork hadn't I discovered yet?

Things Start to Heat Up.

Shortly after the newspaper article came out I was visited by a gentleman at my house who asked if he could speak to me about my art work. He introduced himself as an agent for N C Wyeth, a local established artist.

They both read the newspaper article about my paintings and saw them in a local store window. Asking if I might consider submitting two pieces to exhibit at the Community Center Art Show here in town bought a big smile to my face.

Both were members of the local Art Society and thought that my work was unique and presented an interesting view of the local community in a very artistic way. I was thrilled with the idea and accepted the invitation. The show would be mounted in about 2 weeks and would run for another 2 weeks.

I chose what I thought were my 2 best pictures. One depicted a tiger fighting a bear which I found very dynamic and the other showed a dark cabin in a white cotton field in full bloom with similar puffy white clouds above.

Planning over a good Meal.

Jake suggested a new restaurant across the street from his gallery. It was one I never been to and being early we had no trouble snagging a table. We settled in with wine, ordered dinner and began to discuss a strategy to authenticate the Pippin Painting. I brought him up to date on the latest details such as my visit to the Philadelphia Library, Judith Steins book, her passing along the photo I sent her of the picture to an associate and that person's remarks. I told him about my consequent research concerning the signature and the board origin. I finished by mentioning the contact suggested by Mike and the appraiser/gallery owner offering to look at the painting.

Jake listened intently and allowed me to finish as I checked my notes. He then carefully said, "here is how you should proceed and continue keeping notes and records". At which point I took out a pencil and to write down everything he was saying.

He began to tell me, "drop the scholar she is a non-supporter, the appraiser I know personally, and I would drop him as well", explaining that a friend of his took a painting there for authentication, he was told that that it was not the real deal and somehow the painting was misplaced.

He liked my analysis of the signature thinking it was excellent and very objective. He could see me using my experience as an architect, examining different drawings at different scales to make my point. "Continue this type of analysis of the characteristics exhibited in your bridge painting and you will provide a very convincing argument for authenticity, stay with the supporters and drop the doubters", he exclaimed.

Our entrees were excellent, shrimp for me, venison for Jake and we both had a scrumptious dessert. I made a mental note to recommend "Root", which was the name of the restaurant we were at, to my daughter Laura.

I then presented an idea I had, "I was thinking if I could find the actual covered bridge that was depicted in my Pippin painting placing it in the area he did his work it would help my case".

"Great idea, you mentioned most of his pictures are from Chester County where he lived and that he also may have painted with N C Wyeth, a

Pippin supporter". Many of Wyeth's paintings are also based on Chester County scenes including works along the Brandywine creek".

Jake also suggested that I continue researching all that I can find on Pippin and meticulously begin to pick apart the features of the painting front and back. That way I would have the basics for a convincing report.

Satisfied with the meal and detailed discussion, I toasted Jake with a brandy "to a successful project in finding that this covered bridge picture was painted by Horace Pippin."

Driving back home that night I reflected on my new acquaintance who had hired me to do a drawing for him. Now he was becoming a friend and advisor on this new adventurous project.

Slow Start, Fast Ending.

I was excited but also nervous about entering my pictures in a public show. What if nobody liked my art, what if my paintings were hidden somewhere in the gallery in some dark corner? All these concerns would pass quickly on opening night.

I arrived early to find my two pictures hanging on a brightly lit wall on the third floor. I wondered if anyone would even come all the way up here even though signs read "More Pictures Upstairs". Two other local artists were showing their work up here. A traditional landscape painter with two scenes hanging and a portrait painter showing some nice depictions of family members.

A few visitors arrived at the 6 o'clock scheduled time and by 7:30 the entire 3 floors of galleries were abuzz with over 200 guests. My fears had waned by now for many people were venturing upstairs including reporters from both the local papers and one from Philadelphia.

Later toward the end of the show I had been interviewed by all 3 reporters and photos of my work were taken for possible articles to be printed about the show. Some visitors commented that they liked my paintings for their color, composition and the story that they seemed to portray. I was happy with the feedback in general and was encouraged to spend more time in my studio.

The next morning was a beautiful sunny day and I started it in my garden nursing some early chili pepper plants that I had started from seeds given to me by a friend from Baltimore. The plants had gained strength and stature from the late Spring weather and I was now confident they would bear fruit.

Reading the local paper, I learned that over 1000 visitors had been at the show opening the night before, a record for any exhibit held there at the Community Center. I mused over whether any interest was generated about my two pictures hanging there.

A Dauntless Hunt.

After a few days of catching up with my regular Architecture work, I decided it was time to go searching for the covered bridge in my Pippin painting.

Using Google, I searched for covered bridges in Chester County. This is where Pippin lived and did most of his paintings. Maybe NC Wyeth invited Pippin to accompany him along the Brandywine River to set up and paint at some time. Or perhaps Pippin while traveling or fishing in the streams discovered the bridge along the way. I was surprised that so much information was available about several covered bridges that remained in the West Chester and Coatesville areas either on the Brandywine Creek or one of its many tributaries.

One thing that fascinated me about my painting was the pattern that the roads or paths made. Coming through the bridge from the other side of the stream the road forms a Y each branch going in a different direction. One goes to the left towards the viewer and the other path forks a little to the right going up a hill. The motion depicted in the roads seem to make the picture come alive.

Even though Pippin's work uses very little perspective, these paths add a notion of depth to the scene. Being an architect, I quickly imagined the pattern of the roads from a bird's eye view and made a quick mental sketch of this. This is the pattern I looked for in Google Maps as I put in the location of the several Covered Bridges in Chester county that I had found in the search.

After dismissing three of the aerial views of covered bridges because the roads were straight or on 90-degree angles I finally found a covered bridge with the distinct "Y" shape matching the one in the painting. This bridge was located in Poquoson Township in Chester County was on Frog Hollow Road.

I decided that the next day I would drive there to find the bridge in Horace Pippin's picture. Little did I know that a big adventure awaited me!

The Power of Publicity.

A man by the name of Albert Barnes called me a few days after reading an account of the art show in the Philadelphia Bulletin. I was mentioned as an upcoming folk artist in the West Chester area who had two pieces on exhibit in a local show there. It was enough of a mention to encourage Mr. Barnes, an avid art collector from the Main Line area, to come and see my pictures and ask for my contact info.

"Good morning, I am Albert Barnes wishing to speak to Horace Pippin about one of your paintings at the Community Center", he said as I opened the front door and greeted my visitor. "I am Horace, would you please come in, I am just putting on some coffee", I answered.

After explaining that he was an admirer of fine art and had read about me in the Philadelphia newspaper. He and a friend, N. C. Wyeth, had visited the gallery at the Community Center. "I would be interested in purchasing one of your paintings". He asked me to tell him the story about the Cabin in the Cotton Field picture and what it represented.

I liked this because I always tried to tell a story with my pictures. I explained, "This picture represents the determined nature and hard-working qualities of my people when employed to do a job, the white billowing clouds note hope in obtaining a just wage and the cabin a safe place for rest and family life."

Mr. Barnes liked this story and complimented me on the execution of the painting by offering to purchase it for $200. This being 40 times more than any amount I ever received for a picture made me very happy. I readily accepted his offer and thanked him.

Over coffee and cakes we discussed the idea of a solo show of my work, "would you have about 10 paintings to exhibit at the Art Association where Mr. Wyeth exhibits his work?" he asked. I said that I could have that many pieces ready in about a month or so. My first solo exhibit was scheduled, and I again thanked Mr. Barnes for his help. Leaving on a happy note he said his was looking forward to seeing more of my paintings and wished me a good day.

The Hunt Continues.

Heading out the next morning on a perfectly clear and mild day, I decided to take the scenic route to Chester County and make a day of hunting for the bridge.

I always enjoyed the back roads in this area with their many rolling hills, large horse farms, some small woods and many meadows. There definitely was wealth here, as indicated by the large estate type homes set far back from the white fences lining the roads. This is the country area that the Wyeth family had settled and there were many remarkable stories throughout its history. Reflecting on what I read in Judith Steins book about N C Wyeth being a supporter of Pippin I imagined the two of them looking for painting ideas in this area.

I was finally on Route 82 also known as Doe Run Road, a narrow 2-way country road that offers some fantastic vistas. It was still a mile or two from where I would turn onto McCorkles Rock Road that supposedly lead to the covered bridge.

I have been driving for about 50 years now and considered myself a careful and sometimes cautious driver. Being unfamiliar with this area I was taking my time and obeying the speed limit.

Stopping at a stop sign at the top of an incline I noticed that this was not a cross road but a tee intersection with a road coming in on the left. However, at the stop sign I had difficulty seeing if traffic was approaching from the intersecting road because of the acute angle. So, I proceeded a little more into the intersection, stopping again, affording myself a clear view back over my left shoulder. By now I saw that the road was clear. The only other vehicle in view was a state police car with a trooper at the wheel parked up off the intersecting road cattycorner to me. Thinking this was a bit odd, I proceeded slowly ahead through the clear junction. I was back on track, traveling just below the speed limit, anticipating my destination road to appear soon ahead on my right.

A couple of cars passed me going in the other direction and as I looked in my rear-view mirror, much to my surprise I saw the telltale sign of a police car with lights flashing as it approached behind me. So, I slowed down and at the same time began to make room for the police vehicle to pass. Well that did not happen because now I realized he was signaling for me to pull over and stop. With my right turn signal on I turned onto a narrow road that was on my right. Coming to a stop I realized that this was McCorkles Rock Road. I came to a stop and sat there waiting. How ironic it was that after finally finding my destination I might be prevented from going further.

In the Limelight.

During the next few weeks while I worked hard at finishing the paintings for my upcoming solo show at the Chester County Art Association, I thought about the new possibilities that were opening to me.

Not only would my audience expand past family and friends, but the new exposure could bring more sales and possibly a commission or two from people who might begin to collect my pictures.

Remembering that Dr. Barnes said "The world should see the natural, simple and musical expressions that are exhibited in your paintings" I was determined that the making of my art and the telling of my stories would be my new-found job and ambition.

With this inspiration the 4-week deadline before hanging the show made me work harder than ever in my studio. There were many sleepless nights as I painted to reach my goal of 10 pictures. Using scrap wooden moldings, I constructed rough looking frames attempting to match each picture. Exhausted but satisfied, I got the job done.

Losing at the Wheel.

As the state trooper slowly approached the drive side window, I went over a mental check list. Was my inspection current, do I have my insurance card, what about the vehicle registration? Was I being paranoid? I was probably just anxious because I was on a mission and did not wanted to be detoured.

Doing all the right things, such as keeping both my hands in clear site on the steering wheel, I noticed this trooper was very young. Maybe he was a recently graduated cadet from the Academy, I thought, as he instructed me to open the window. Maybe I was his first catch!

After taking my cards and returning to his cruiser and spending what seemed like an eternity there, he finally came back and said, "I suppose you are wondering why I pulled you over?". I had no idea, I was honoring the speed limit, I think my van is operating correctly and I have all my paper work up to date.

"I am giving you a citation for failing to stop at a stop sign" he said confidentially". My jaw dropped, and I was speechless, my expression must have surprised him because he took a step backwards. Not knowing what to say I just stared at him. As if his accusation was not enough. He continued by saying, "not only did you jump the stop sign you also sped away from the intersection after you noticed my car sitting there."

I took a deep resolved breath and carefully responded, "no officer that is not the case, I actually stopped twice and slowly proceeded when I could clearly see that no other traffic was coming"! Failing to consider what I said, the trooper proceeded to hand me a ticket for 175 dollars and read my rights about appealing, etc.

As if this was not enough he continued, "what are you doing in this neighborhood, so far away from your home in Fleetwood?" Knowing that this was a lost battle I replied, "I am an architect interested in the history of buildings and I was looking for a covered bridge close by."

Eyeing me as if I was someone who was a career thief casing this very expensive and exclusive neighborhood, he told me to be more careful with my driving habits and left me there, stupefied.

Joining the Art World.

Up to now my sketches, pictures and few paintings were not seen beyond the town limits that I live in. All this was about to change with my first solo show.

The Chester County Art Association reached far and wide. Members such as N.C. Wyeth, Howard Pyle and many other distinguished artists as well as patrons such as the DuPont family and Dr. Albert Barnes made this place a bastion of what the Art World is about.

Many museum curators would come from afar to view work, buy pieces and learn of promising new artists on the scene. News of my show already had spread to Philadelphia and New York with museums and galleries inquiring about my work. The newspaper reporters were already advertising the show as "A New Folk Artist rises in West Chester". All this buzz added to the anticipation of the opening reception.

Having some experience from the Community Center show I knew to dress well and be there before hand to receive guests as they arrived. Being a solo show, my pictures had been hung in the expansive gallery on the first floor of the Association building which was an historic wooden building dating over a hundred years old. It reminded me of some of the Southern Mansions I viewed in various publications.

It was only 30 minutes since the doors opened and the gallery was overflowing with guests. The rooms were filled, and other guests waited in the halls and anterooms waiting to come view my paintings.

Pushing on.

Not one to be easily deterred I slowly proceeded along the stone path that I had turned onto. After all, this was McCorkles Rock Road and there was a covered bridge ahead of me to find.

The road lead me past a very large farm on my left and several small meadows on the right. Ahead of me I viewed rolling hills with lots of trees. I turned my attention to the beautiful spring day, not a single cloud in the sky, and began to look for Buck Run where the bridge was supposed to be located.

About a half mile along I came to a small gravel parking lot for about 8-10 cars and a sign post displaying "Laurels Preserve" with smaller writing below that I could not read from my vehicle. There were two empty cars parked here and I pulled into an empty space. I next inspected the sign post where I read, Brandywine Conservancy, open only to members. To the right of the sign a wide dirt path began, parallel to a quick running stream. An unlocked closed gate gave access to the trail head. Additional information on the sign listed a phone number and website where one could join The Brandywine Conservancy.

Still having a cell phone signal, I dialed the number only to receive a voice message to visit the Brandywine River Art museum for more information. I next tried the website, but my signal was not strong enough to connect. I returned to my van thinking that I would have to come back another time to go bridge hunting.

My mind turned back to the bad police experience I just had and this made me get out of the car and return to the unlocked gate. I thought to myself, "I just drove two hours to get here, survived a state trooper encounter and I attempted to join the conservancy so I would not be deterred from proceeding on my hunt. Going through the gate, as the stream widened flanked by towering rocks and woods on my right, I began once again to enjoy a magnificent day.

An Exciting Encounter.

Making my way through the crowd saying hello and answering questions I noticed that some of my pictures had little red dots below them. "I see you made some sales", a voice from behind me whispered. Turning I greeted Dr. Barnes, "Thank you for arranging this show and for coming to the opening", I responded.

He went on to explain that the red dots signified paintings sold and that he had added to his collection the picture with the fox in the snow-covered field. "This must be a record crowd for a show, I cannot remember one with so many visitors on opening night, you should mingle and meet as many people as possible". Taking his que, I headed over to a corner where a well-dressed lady was studying one of my favorite paintings.

It was her bright red scarf that had caught my attention and as I approached she turned and gave me a big smile.

"Good evening, thank you for coming to my show, my name is Horace Pippin", I said with a warm welcome. Turning back to the picture she asked, "Are the houses that you painted in this picture located here in here in town?".

The picture was about 24 inches by 18 inches tall and it depicted 5 brick row homes with small front yards in which flowers and trees grew. Just off center in one of the yards an enormous tree reached high toward the bright blue sky. The entire scene was topped with puffy white clouds floating peacefully across the sky.

Responding in an admiring way, "I painted a picture of the brick homes down the street from where I live because I always loved the pattern of the bricks and that big tree always told a story to me, do you like this picture"?

She came a little closer to me and said, "I find it very interesting, captivating, colorful and puzzling all at the same time", she exclaimed". Continuing she said, "I cannot figure out why there are two distinct types of leaves on the same tree"?

Responding I said, "Good question, all my pictures tell a story and this one tells a very simple but serious one.

A Pair of Covered Bridges.

About a half mile or so along the trail I encountered an older gentleman and dog, we greeted and continued in opposite directions. I was thinking to myself why there were not more people enjoying this beautiful landscape. I guessed that the land probably belonged to a wealthy family who had donated money to the Conservancy, so it could be preserved and enjoyed by its members. Not feeling the least like a trespasser, since I intended to become a member when I got home I continued following the winding path.

About half mile along where the trail rose above the twisting stream I caught a glimpse of a red fox in the distance and a large hawk closer by. The landscape was now changing. The stream became wider, the rocky bank gave way to more level land revealing brighter meadows and pastures.

As I turned onto one of these meadows on my right I spotted a covered bridge. My excitement made me pick up my pace as I hurried ahead to take a closer look. My demeanor quickly turned to disappointment because I began to realize this was not the bridge in the painting.

This covered bridge formed a 90-degree angle with the path I was on and the bridge was much longer than the one depicted in this picture. Lost in the bridge's dim interior I stopped halfway across and wondered if I made a mistake trying to find the subject of the painting. Would it be like trying to find a needle in a hay stack?

I turned around not making the trip across the stream. Back on the path I took out my cell phone and using Google maps I was able to pinpoint my current location.

Google maps is amazing because I have found that even with a poor signal I still can access this amazing GPS tool on my phone and bring up a satellite view of the surrounding landscape. I imagined hundreds of google satellites circling overhead beaming directions to my little device.

I was not surprised at the image on the phone. A blue dot noted my current location at the 90-degree intersection of two roads with a tag that read Speakman Bridge No. 1.

Being my curious self, I tapped the photo image feature which gave me a bird's eye view of my surroundings. The lush green tree tops were in view as well as the red painted roof of this bridge. Zooming out using two fingers on the screen I hoped to spot where I parked my vehicle.

"Wait, what is that?" I said out loud to myself. I noticed that another bridge appeared at the top of my screen. Totally excited I practically raced back across this bridge and headed in the direction of the second one.

The Row House Story.

In a very serious tone with a captive audience of one charming lady, I told my story of the Row Houses. "This painting shows the houses on the block here in town where I live". I went on to explain that the gardens featured in the front yards highlight my interest in planting seeds each year and watching the flowers and vegetables grow throughout the summer and autumn. The brick homes illustrate the careful pattern of the bricks, the time and skill required by masons who created the walls.

I always like to use a splash of red in my pictures and that is why the male cardinal is sitting on the front branches of the big tree.

"In answer to your question about the different leaves on the one tree, they are the leaves of the catalpa and pin oak trees. The elephant ear size of the catalpa leaves provides great shade during the summer days and to me they hide prejudices that still exist here in this community".

"The pin oak leaves stay on all winter only to be shed the following spring representing the patience that I exhibit to overcome the feelings of unacceptance. The bright sky and shining clouds exhibit my hopes of seeing my dreams come true."

Thinking I may have been a bit over bearing, I said, "I hope I have not overwhelmed you explaining all my feelings that come out with this painting".

Subject of Picture Found.

Proceeding along the path and totally excited, I came to another clearing with a second covered bridge in view. It was smaller in length then the first bridge and was situated against a back ground of trees rising to a nearby low ridge. I immediately ran ahead to a vantage point that mimicked the view in the painting. Spanning a bend in Doe Run creek this bridge shouted out to me, here it was, connecting 3-paths in a "Y" shape, exactly as I remembered from my first look on my computer at home. There was also an old abandoned dirt path that I imagined lead to a home or farm rising the hill to the left. That would explain the open mailbox in the painting. Here, many years ago someone would walk down to collect their mail.

There were newer trees about 20-30 years old that had sprung up in front of the bridge now. However, all the other landscape features matched the painting exactly. "I found the bridge that Horace Pippin had painted", I said out loud to myself.

I imagined a scene where Pippin stood either making a hand sketch or perhaps with his easel set up he started to create a wonderful little painting. After taking many photos with my phones camera I had a feeling of satisfaction and excitement that made this trip today worthwhile.

Returning on the same path, I crossed the first bridge and thought that despite getting stopped by the cop, receiving an undeserved ticket and almost turning back at the gate to the path because of non-membership requirements I accomplished today's goal after all.

The parking area was empty, I've been here for over three hours. I took a picture of the sign post before getting back into my vehicle and headed home. I could not wait to compare my Pippin painting with the photos of the covered bridge that I had found.

Another Collector of My Art.

"Not at all Mr. Pippin, I appreciate your forth coming story and the honesty that goes into your work, particularly this painting", she exclaimed!

This mysterious lady then surprised me by saying, "I would like to purchase this painting if it is for sale, I would find it a wonderful addition to my bedroom opposite a window where the early morning sun greets me".

"Please call me Horace", I stuttered while thanking her for appreciating my art as well as giving this painting a new home.

" I am so thrilled to meet you Horace, my name is Mary Ann Pyle, I am not exactly a neighbor but I live close enough, only a few miles south of town". "But now I feel closer because of you sharing your story and your art with me".

Mary Ann went on to say she lived with her sister Sally and father. Our farm is about halfway towards Coatesville close to Doe Run a popular fishing stream. "We raise horses and I would love for you to come visit sometime". Continuing she said that is was a beautiful area with many places that might inspire me in my future art work.

Not knowing how to respond and feeling a bit flushed I took her out stretched hand and responded, "thank you for the invitation and your purchase of my painting". I explained that I would come visit sometime in the future for I was always looking for interesting scenes to sketch and paint.

Mary Ann smiled broadly and urged me to circulate amongst the other guests for they came to see my work and learn about me, the new exciting artist who lived here in town. On leaving she turned and said, "please put a red dot on the Row House painting for it had been sold".

Making the Connection.

Being an architect, I find the computer indispensable when it comes to doing drawings. Whether I am designing a home, a new toy or even comparing the photo of an object to a similar image depicted in a painting it is so handy in getting the job done.

The next day I was printing out a large poster size drawing showing two images, first a photo of the painting at the top and below a construction of a super imposed photograph of the actual bridge. With three colored lines I outlined the main geometric compositions of the painting showing that there was no doubt that this was the bridge in the painting.

Having now found the subject of the Pippin picture, I went into research mode, looking for the bridge's history. I also was curious to find out why Horace Pippin painted this scene.

Ironically Pippin was born about the same time the bridge was constructed in the 1880s. I found that Pippin was the only child of a poor family in a small town, finding it difficult to make ends meet.

The bridge was one of two built by a successful farmer and merchant, John Pyle, who named this bridge after one of his daughters, Mary Ann. The bridge was located between two populated villages, West Chester where Pippin lived and Coatesville south of there, which supported a bustling industrial community.

It was a beautiful rural district with a few families that owned large plots of land. This area was well known to established artists. An area that offered endless vistas of meadows, streams, knolls, barns, wildlife, all popular subjects for painting.

Later I was to learn that NC Wyeth through his agent would be shown some of Pippin's artwork that was displayed in local stores. Along with Albert Barnes a collector they encouraged Pippin to show at popular galleries helping him rise quickly in art world.

The Aftermath.

The show proved to be an enormous success with 10 of 18 paintings being sold. I made more money in one night than I had earned in the previous year.

As I sat alone at the kitchen table the next morning foremost in my mind was Mary Ann's warm departure and her invitation to come paint at her place sometime.

Jannette had been gone for a few weeks helping take care of her sister who never quite recovered from a bout of pneumonia this past winter. Although Aunt Sally was making progress it was my wife who was having trouble. The medicine she was taking for depression was now becoming addictive and its benefits were wearing off. I worried about both.

With the newspaper opened to the review of last night's opening, I could not help from smiling and thinking how my new career in art was finally happening.

The article gave a complimentary review mentioning how a record crowd had turned out at the Community Center to welcome Horace Pippin and view his paintings and that 10 paintings had been sold. Dr. Albert Barnes had purchased 3 of them for his galleries.

Reflecting on the invitation to visit Mary Ann, I wondered how and when I would be able to make the trip to her place. In the meantime, though much had to be planned. Mr. Wyeth's agent had mentioned that a show of my work was now being planned for his gallery in Philadelphia.

It would be necessary to have a dozen new paintings finished in the next two months in addition to one ones that had not sold. The aftermath of my successful show was twofold, positive recognition with some serious collectors coming forth contrasted with the pressure to perform at a rate I was not used to.

The Report.

After brainstorming with Jake on what to do next to have the picture authenticated, I decided to write a report. Although the current name for the bridge was Speakman Bridge #2, I named the painting "The Mary Ann Pyle Bridge". While I was gathering my notes from reading Judith Stein's book for a second time I sent another email to her scholar friend along with the comparison photos of the painting and the actual bridge.

Her reply was brief, "finding the subject of one's work is always a good thing, I may forward your email to a friend at the Met Museum of art in NYC who is also familiar with Pippin". That would be the last I would hear from her.

Meeting again with Jake In Philadelphia a few days later, I related my experience of finding the actual bridge in the painting. Studying the poster highlighting the comparison photos of painting and bridge, Jake told me, "you are doing all the right things, continue the clever work and you will develop a compelling case toward authentication".

I responded, "I have this idea of writing a sort of academic type report, very objective in nature, highlighting my findings and then mailing it to museums offering the painting as a loaner for exhibition, what do you think?"

"Can't hurt", he said, "instead of emailing your report why not send it the old fashion way?" "Type it up, print it out, add photos and snail mail it".

New Developments.

I began to work furiously to meet the deadline set for my next show, my first one in Philadelphia. There was little time for my mind to wander. I had not heard any more about Jannette's health other than the fact that she was now being cared for in an assisted living facility along with her sister Sally who had been admitted with a worsening condition.

Being alone and working night and day, my mind would occasionally wander back to the opening night meeting with Mary Ann and her interest in my work. Hadn't she invited me to her farm? How would I ever learn where she lived?

By now, Dr. Barnes's art agent was calling me almost daily. "How many paintings are finished for the show? Are the new ones varied in content? Will you be able to show 25 or more, I need to fill the gallery walls".

As the deadline approached my confidence grew from not only assembling the requested quota of pictures but by the quality and content of my new art work. I drew again from my WWI experiences, from historic events in the lives of figures before and after the Civil War, from church related experiences to happenings in and around my town. There were so many stories that my heart could tell I thought I could paint for the rest of my life.

I saw my dream of being an accomplished artist coming true. I was now recognized not only around town, but stories of my pictures were now appearing in magazines and newspapers in many cities. Several museums were inquiring about the possibility of showing my work in special exhibits.

The president of the Chester County Art Association became a major supporter. He arranged a 6-piece show at MOMA, Museum of Modern Art in NYC. This show was so well publicized and attended that I now became a national figure in the art world. Then alarming news came from upstate New York.

Following Through.

Jake had said, "Be concise, be objective, follow the supporters". "You already have several key factors to substantiate your find, add another 6 and you will be ready to mail it off to museums".

My initial list included, the National Gallery of Art in DC, Philadelphia Museum of Art, PAFA, the Barnes Museum, Brandy River Art Museum and Delaware Museum of Art. These were chosen for being close to Pippin's home and because of associations with some of the people who supported him.

Early that evening I began to read Judith's book again. Looking for new clues I found that Pippin would sometimes cut larger canvas boards to use for several paintings. He could not afford the stretchers and canvas that most artists used for their work.

Measuring the board used for my bridge picture I found it to be exactly 24" long and 14 ½" tall. Since I had to do the measuring on the back because of the frame hiding the true edge, I noticed something new. This canvas board had been cut very neatly along the 24" dimension. Here was one of these pieces from a larger board. I clearly now saw 3 factory edges where the canvas tucks tightly around the edge of the board foundation. The cut was so good that it would easily been missed by a casual glance, as I had first done.

I wondered out loud, "what are the common sizes of canvass boards?" A quick search brought up a list of about standard board sizes including 24" x 24" and one that was 24" x 36". Cutting a 14 ½" x 24" board (the bridge painting size) from this larger board would leave a remnant of 24" x 21 ½".

Continuing to read, Judith cites an example of a painting on such a cut down canvas board being the portrait of the "Chester County Art Critic". Flipping back to the index I found the page for this picture and to my amazement found that the size of the Art Critic was 16" x 21 ½" tall. A perfect match leaving an 8 "strip of canvas board as a 3rd remnant. "And what do you think"? I found 2 more canvas board works measuring exactly 8" wide by 10" or so tall. I never would had imagined that Pippin using a standard 24"x 36" board would paint 4 individual pictures one of which was the Covered Bridge picture. I sat back and sighed, "this detective work is really paying off".

As a young kid a friend and I read all the Hardy Boys mysteries and fashioned we as an agency solving capers. We would hide, like Pippin did, under porches of row homes and listen for clues as people passed by.

A Very Sad Time.

Riding the roller coaster of success and attention, my shows, museum requests and now commissions were bringing I assumed all would be ok in upstate New York with my wife and aunt.

I could have not been further from the truth. Having arrived at the train station with no one to greet me, I began to feel a dark cloud gathering. Expecting to be greeted by Jannette, I found myself alone on the platform on a cool cloudy morning. I took a cab to Aunt Sally's only to find a distant cousin minding the house. He told me Aunt Sally had died from a stroke related to her heart condition and her sister was at a nearby institution receiving rehab for drug overdose.

How could all of this have happened in such a brief time? I was so caught up in my instant successes and looming deadlines that I lost tract of family and friends.

Some More Clues.

I kept repeating to myself, "What did the scholar mean by the comment that the signature is way out of scale with the painting, so it was not a Pippin?", as I continued to research Pippin's work.

So I decided to evaluate the signature size on most of his pictures. This was not all that difficult because the book not only show images of Pippin's paintings it also gave their overall sizes. Again, using my cad program, I uploaded the images to their full size and began to measure the height of the letters in the signatures.

I quickly found that in all cases Pippin's signature measured very closely to a common ½" height. Going to my painting I measured the signature and it was ½" tall.

And then it hit me. When looking at a smaller painting displayed in Stein's book the ½" high letters would appear relatively big in comparison to canvass size and in the larger boards such as the Art Critic painting the same ½" signature would seem to be much smaller. The pictures in the book were not scaled relative to each other, so it would be possible for one to think that Pippin used many different letter sizes when signing his work.

I again reviewed the format of Pippin's signature as pointed out in Stein's book. This being H. PiPPiN., with the letters in a combination of these upper and lower cases. This is exactly the way the signature appears on my Mary Ann Pyle Bridge painting.

A Grieving Time.

Losing Aunt Sally was a big loss, but nothing prepared me for the grief I felt when Jannette passed away. I had been visiting her every day for two weeks when she succumbed to what was noted as insanity.

On the first visit I barely recognized her from her loss of weight and grayness in her appearance that was more chilling then a late autumn stormy cloud. The doctors told me that she had tried to take her life with a stolen scissor.

She was now so heavily medicated that I was not remembered by her and her speech was not discernable, almost as if she also had a stroke. The chair she was slumped in seem to all but gobble her up.

On a rare occasion during my visits she would shout out "where is my boy with those bombs, guns and knives?"

I was so horrified by her condition that it brought back vivid memories of the agony I experienced in the trenches during the Great War. With no recovery to be hoped for I only wished she would escape her tormented existence.

Not being able to help I returned home with a sense of loss to be replaced by the heavy grief brought on by news of her death.

Museum Time.

With more solid evidence for my report in hand, I decided it was time to visit the museums in the area that listed paintings by Horace Pippin in their collections. Up to now I only had my painting which was yellowed with age and had some paint missing near the signature and the pictures of his art in the books I have been reading as reference to Pippin's work.

Since Pippin was from Chester County and N. C. Wyeth one of his early supporters, I headed to the Brandywine River Art Museum which is a bastion for works by the Wyeth's and close to where Pippin lived and painted. After all I had found the bridge in my painting nearby at Laurel Preserves. A very large exhibit of Pippin's works was exhibited here in 1976 in a show curated by Judith Stein.

As I drove past the intersection where I previously encountered the State Trooper during my search for the bridge I could not help but to laugh to myself how that day turned around.

Arriving at the museum I remembered how I had been here before when I was in Architecture school. An old barn had been converted into a small museum for displaying local art works. It now had grown with several wings tastefully added to maintain a rustic but modern look. I had been here on a field visit to study the design concept at that time to offer inspiration to a design project we were assigned.

Entering the building I was greeted by an elderly woman who asked if I was a member. I gladly joined with an annual membership knowing I would return and probably again visit the Conservancy where the bridge was built. There were also many events throughout the year that were open to members only.

Inquiring about paintings by Horace Pippin I learned presently only two were on exhibit, perhaps sometime soon several of his other works that the Museum had would come on display.

Climbing the circular stair to the upper gallery where the paintings were hung I imagined the excitement that must have prevailed during the big show years ago when most of the known Pippin paintings were being shown.

By now having studied most of the pictures in Judith Stein's book I was able to quickly spot the two Pippin paintings.

Both of these paintings were about 25% smaller in total size than my bridge painting. The colors were very bright and vibrant since the pictures most likely had been cleaned and restored. This made me wonder how my painting would look if it was also conserved. I thought of the yellowed snow in my bridge painting and the chipped paint. I said to myself, "the blue in the grey sky would begin to come out and the snow would be much whiter, and I bet some green color would be revealed in those dark black trees on the left of my painting."

I began to realize that when the time came, finding the right conservator for my painting would be very important. I had heard of some bad experiences that friends had with their paintings being ruined because of improper handling of art they had given to restorers during the treatment process.

Remembering what I had read in Stein's book that because of the nature of the materials that Pippin used, conservation might be very difficult. The house paints and various foundations that he used were susceptible to wearing poorly and might be damaged when cleaned.

The two Pippin pictures on display currently were very beautiful, however the subjects were different than that in my picture. However, the size and format in both signatures matched exactly that on my bridge painting.

My inquiry about other Pippin works was answered by the guide, "the Museum has many works done by him, but they are in storage at the current time". I learned that just 6 months ago the museum had many more of his works on display in a show that was greatly received. I thought to myself, "maybe the next time my bridge picture would be alongside some of those".

A Brighter Note

With much support and prompting from friends, supporters and agents I returned to my studio and furiously got back to producing my art.

And then the letter arrived, answering my dreams of Mary Ann's invitation. It was an early spring morning with the promise of a warning sun. Birds where happily singing on the boughs instead of scurrying about for something to eat.

As I sat at the kitchen table over coffee and my usual two eggs over easy, a knock on the rear door followed by a warm greeting, "good morning Horace, fine day out here, you should come and paint", the mailman came in and handed me the post.

Among the letters was a large envelope addressed to: Mr. Horace Pippin, care of the Chester County Art Association. Thinking this odd, because most galleries or museums usually addressed me directly, I hastily opened it.

Inside I found another sealed colorful envelope addressed, Horace Pippin, with a return address in the upper left corner, Mary Ann Pyle, Laurel Preserves, Chester County. The writing was in a beautiful cursive format reminding me of calligraphy.

My heart skipped a beat as I quietly said to myself, "was this Mary Ann's invitation to for me to visit her?". Inside the second envelope were a dried pressed flower of a Mountain Laurel bloom which was the State flower, along with two letters.

The first letter was a request for me to consider doing a commissioned portrait of Mary Ann riding her new horse, a black stallion. The other letter was two pages long and was quite personal, even a bit intimate. The content surprised me, but I welcomed the intention it seemed to indicate.

In the same beautiful calligraphy lettering it read, "My dear Horace, I cannot thank you enough for the wonderful picture that I purchased at your show when I meet you. Late that night I hung it on the wall opposite my bed next to a window that receives the morning sun. As I awake each day I am somewhat aroused by staring at it and remembering the story that the picture tells."

"All of the beautiful features that it exhibits are so clear to me, and viewing the painting seems to expose new emotions each time I study it. I am truly grateful for having meet you and learning insights on how you go about creating your art. I will enjoy it for the rest of my life and will somehow find a better way of expressing my thanks.

Please consider my request to sit for a private commission soon. I am enclosing my return address and I look forward to your response. Very Warmly yours, Mary Ann."

I felt a rush of heat, I was very excited to hear from Mary Ann and I took the package and contents as a blessing that would help me find my way out of my grief and darkness.

More Museum Visits.

Having grown up in Philadelphia and teaching Architecture at CCP for a long time gave me an advantage for my next museum visits. I knew exactly where to go and what to look for at the PAFA, Philadelphia Art Museum and the Barnes Foundation, all of which I planned to visit on my trip.

The PAFA, Pennsylvania Academy of Fine Arts, building is one of my favorites in Philadelphia. Designed by Frank Furness it has adorned the corner of Broad and Cherry Streets since the late 1800's. While in Architectural School I remember it from many of the annual Beaux Arts parties hosted there. My sister attended classes there and learned how to paint. My Dad worked part time as a docent in the galleries there after his retirement from Boeing.

Horace Pippin taught some classes there. The gallery that started his movement to success was located nearby. It must have been very fulfilling for Pippin, having his art displayed here and for sale at the gallery down the street. He shared his philosophy on art as detailed in the book, "I Tell My Heart" which describes the essence of his paintings.

Several of his works are in PAFA collections and there is always one on display. One painting I am viewing here today is titled "Abe Lincoln, The Good Samaritan". It is also a snow scene and I study the brush strokes, noting the similarity to those in my bridge painting. The composition and geometry of the block shapes are also alike.

Next on the schedule was the Philadelphia Museum of Art. I learned from the books I read that Pippin's painting "The Art Critic of Chester County" was here. This was the painting that was on canvas board cut from a larger common size panel 24"x36" with the remnant piece used for my bridge picture. I did not expect to see the back of the Art Critic painting but was interested in studying the composition up close. Much to my disappointment I found that the painting had been put into storage. The receptionist informed that in less than a year a show titled Modern Times would be on exhibit with 3 Pippins on display. She gladly issued me a refund and welcomed me to return for the upcoming show.

Dreams Come True.

Early on a brilliant spring Saturday I set out to visit Mary Ann. With my sketch materials strapped to the back of my bicycle I could hardly contain my excitement.

The invitation arrived on Monday the same week, "My dear Horace, Daddy has agreed to you painting my portrait here at our farm, I am so excited to think that you will visit and see my new black stallion. He says you should come on Saturday about noon. He can discuss terms of the commission and you can do your study sketches in the afternoon.

It is my greatest wish that you accept the invitation for I have been dreaming of seeing you again since our meeting at the art show.

To get here follow the main road towards Coatesville and turn off at the junction that takes you to Doe Run. From there look for the second covered bridge and turn up the left lane before crossing the bridge. There is a large mail box at the junction of the two paths reading Speakman Farm. I am anxiously looking forward to seeing you, Yours Truly. Mary Ann.

All week I had wondered if my memory had served me correctly. Was she as pretty as I remembered, had her eyes sparkled when I shared the stories that my paintings told? Had her parting handshake not only been firm but also convey a warm and endearing feeling to it?

I guessed these questions would soon be answered as I got off my bicycle to walk it up the very steep hill to her farm. I was a bit nervous.

The Barnes Foundation.

Dr. Albert C Barnes a very successful and wealthy mainliner amassed a $25 billion collection of fine art and for decades displayed them at his mansion outside of Philadelphia.

Today the collection is located at the Barnes Museum just down the street from the Philadelphia Museum of Art. The strikingly modern design was in great contrast to his old historic house and foundation where he lived. I have been wanting to visit the Barnes Museum since it was completed four years ago. Now I had an extra incentive to do so. On display there were 4 paintings by Horace Pippin that Dr. Barnes had purchased early in the artist's career.

It was Dr. Barnes along with N.C. Wyeth who supported Pippin and sponsored his first major show at the Chester County Art Association in the early 1940's.

Dr. Barnes took a liking to Pippin and invited him to join the foundation's school for upcoming artists. The exposure to the diversity of art by the world masters on display there had an influence on many of Pippin's future works.

As I approached the museum I remembered the many field trips my Architecture students and I made here to observe the construction and finally enjoy the design of the finished building and beautifully landscaped entrance.

Once inside I was surprised by the interior layout. Then I remembered that part of the deal of moving Dr. Barnes' collection here was to have all the paintings remain in the exact relative location that they had been in his old mansion. The galleries were small with lofty ceilings, the finishes and wood trim matched those that were prevalent when his home was built. In each room there were many paintings, some high off the floor, all neatly arranged to give each work its own space.

The Pippin's were in two different rooms. As I studied them I imagined a young Horace Pippin explaining to the Doctor the story behind each of his pictures. I looked carefully at the composition of each work and the way Pippin would layer colors on top of each other to achieve a desired effect as Judith Stein had explained in her book. Taking pictures was allowed if no flash was used, so I took close ups of the brush strokes and the strong geometric shapes Pippin used in his compositions.

On the way home, that evening I felt a sense of accomplishment, a little more research and I would be able to complete the report on my bridge painting.

A Deal Sealed.

Standing on the porch of the house across from the barn stood a stern looking man about twice my age. "Greetings", he shouted, "you must be the artist that Mary Ann mentioned". I was about to answer when a mounted horse came from around the back of the barn, it was a beautiful black stallion with an even more beautiful lady riding him. Mary Ann sat perfectly straight commanding quite a pose. Her ample bosom filled the pink blouse she was wearing, her legs were bronze and very taut. She bought the horse around at a slow but steady gait and dismounted in a single sweeping motion.

A huge smile crossed her face as she caught me staring opened mouth. "Good morning Mr. Pippin", she exclaimed with a furtive glance in her daddy's direction, "I am so glad you found us on this glorious day". By now a bit agitated her daddy started back into the house saying, "please start with the portrait and when finished stop in to discuss the terms and schedule to complete the painting".

The next 3 hours were most enjoyable as Mary Ann and her horse pranced about taking on many poses. First across the red barn wall, then the stone wall, and finally in front of the dark expanse at the opened barn doors. Working hard at my sketches I was able to assemble over a dozen studies. I came alongside the stallion as Mary Ann prepared to dismount. She took my offered hand and warmly stroked it as she said, "Thank you Horace, I have been dreaming of you here making your pictures". "I cannot wait to see your portrait of me and I plan to hang it in my bedroom opposite of the Rowhouse painting I purchased from you.

Having returned to the porch Daddy beckoned us over so he could formally meet Horace. Light handshakes were exchanged, and he thanked me for coming. We agreed on $200 for the portrait and he asked that it be mailed before the *end of the summer because Mary Ann and her sister Sally would be traveling to Europe for an extensive journey.*

If her daddy were not present I would have given Mary Ann a warm embrace. She did not take her eyes off mine. We bid our goodbyes and I headed home cycling hard to beat the oncoming dusk.

Research Continues.

The next few days were devoted to Judith Stein's book, each time I would learn more about Pippin and his art. The chapter titled "Materials and Techniques" would offer invaluable information on how Pippin painted with several new clues to help support my findings.

Forgeries of Pippin's work is discussed in this chapter. Basically, two types exist, those that try to imitate his style and subject matter and those that are primitive in nature with Pippin's signature added. Judith mentions that his fakes are easy to spot because of their uncharacteristic subjects, unusual supports and a paint application that fails to imitate the laborious layering and distinctive brush work Pippin used. The characteristics of my bridge painting were no doubt those exhibited in a true Pippin and not in a copied or fake one.

The chapter continues to explain, Pippin often used layering of assorted colors to achieve special effects. Rather than simply refining a color's value, he often created a completely different hue. Pippin's portrait of Paul B. Dague, Deputy Sheriff of Chester County (1937) illustrates this with the various blue and blue-gray colors under the bright yellow background. The same effect is evident in "Saturday Night Bath" on the top part of the rear wall.

In my bridge painting the sky to the right side of the canvas board shows these exact characteristics and on the rear of the board along the edge of this area the different layers of paint are seen clearly. Judith makes a point of this effect being present on the rear of the paintings where the assorted colors would bleed over. An example giving is "The Getaway" painting (1939), where she states, "On the reverse (rear or back of the support) there is more evidence of the brighter blue colors of the sky than are now visible on the front and red under layers to what are yellow gray clouds.

Another supporting clue for my bridge painting report came from Jen Bryant's book "A Splash of Red". Jen writes, "Every day and late into the night, Horace (Pippin) worked on his painting. He used gray, black and white, the somber colors of war. Here and there he added a splash of red." In my bridge painting most of the colors are subdued or somewhat somber, however a splash of red occurs as the flag on the mailbox.

More Work.

My summer turned into a whirlwind of events. With a growing number of requests from museums, galleries and collectors for my work I had difficulty keeping up with the demand. I would spend many sleepless nights in my studio as I worked straight through to the next morning.

A recent show in Philadelphia at Carlen Galleries got the attention of a Time Magazine reporter who did a cover story on me. My painting "Cabin in Cotton" was on the cover. Dr. Barnes had purchased it a while ago and now it's value would sky rocket. All my paintings displayed sold and Dr. Barnes suggested to the dealer that my prices be raised considerable for future shows. It was interesting that later he refused to buy any of my paintings at these higher prices and he did not acquire another Pippin after 1943.

While I studied at the Barnes Foundation I became to appreciate that his father was injured during the Civil War and had an arm amputated, a fate that easily could have happened to me. Sickness shortened my studies at the Barnes and an ever more demanding schedule of shows allowed me to do nothing but paint.

A show at the prestigious gallery Bignon in New York City resulted from a recommendation by Barnes as did a nomination for a Guggenheim Fellowship for me to travel to the Southern States to capture the lives of African Americans living in that region. I was passed over for this project since the reward went to another artist. He next recommended me to have a show at the San Francisco Museum of Art along with the work of an artist by the name Settanni. Only one of my paintings was selected, however a year later the museum director Grace McCann Morley organized a solo show of my work.

How I Paint.

I was approaching the goal of finding a dozen supporting clues for my bridge painting report, by studying more examples of Pippin's paintings. The following two indicators of Pippin's art come from Judith Stein. "In Pippin's early works the palette tends towards simple, often muted color combinations", and from Dorothy Miller quoting Pippin, "How I Paint; the colors are simple such as brown, amber, yellow, black, white and green".

Evidence of both remarks are in my bridge painting where the sky, background hills, trees and the roof of the bridge come together.

My research was coming to an end. At this point I had much proof that my Mary Ann Bridge painting had been painted by Horace Pippin. So as not to be redundant, I decided to stop gathering evidence and write my findings in an objective and definitive report to share with others.

Finding Time.

At the expense of many sleepless nights I still found time to complete the portrait of Mary Ann on her horse in front of the barn. Packing it carefully in a wooden crate I mailed it along with an invoice to her father.

I wished I could deliver it in person because I still had a strong attraction to Mary Ann and I wished to explain to her how the painting came together. Based on the cool reception and delivery request by her father I decided it best to honor his wishes.

During the next couple of weeks I found the time to set up my easel about town. One day in front of the Chester County Court House I was busy sketching an outline of a new painting.

Having ambivalent feelings on law and justice, the system of administering the law in a fair and unbiased way always fascinated me. A good many of my pictures address questions that arise when I look at the outcomes of our legal system.

My pictures "The Hanging of John Brown", my Abe Lincoln paintings as well as the Court House I just begun, all stir up emotions that bring me back to my WWI days and the senseless injustices that I often experienced.

Old Glory was flying in front of the Court House and it's intent was what inspired this painting. And some of the dark shadows I bring out question whether justice is being administered fairly? This is how I explained the picture to Sheriff Paul Dague one afternoon as he stopped to watch me finish the painting.

Having introduced himself a few days earlier he mentioned, "I very much enjoyed your past show at the

Community Center". Paul went on to say he wanted to meet me that night, however an intense discussion between a beautiful lady and myself prevented it.

He invited me to have dinner with him that weekend. There we discussed the challenges of his job and how I could find refuge in my paintings. Paul asked me to do a portrait of him. Agreeing, we meet several more times, mostly at his house where he opened up to me and asked if I would consider being closer. At first, I thought it was totally unacceptable but later wondered what it would be like to love another man? The relationship may have developed except for my extremely busy schedule and the arrival of a very intimate letter from Mary Ann.

Report Finished and Mailed.

The report of my findings came together rather easily because of careful note taking, saving pictures and writing about the various discussions I had with people I meet during my investigation of Pippin's life and work.

My 2-year plan concerning my Pippin project had been to authenticate the painting and loan it to a museum for display. I also wished to write a book about my experiences in this process, entwined with a short fictional biography of Horace Pippin. Even though a full year had passed, I believed that I was somewhat on schedule.

I composed a cover letter, made a list of museums to write to and formatted my findings into a 21-page report of text and sample pictures. It was very professional, easy to read and presented a very good case that my Mary Ann Pyle Bridge picture was indeed painted by Horace Pippin.

The next day I mailed the enclosures to: Barnes Foundation, Philadelphia Museum of Art, PAFA, Brandywine River Art Museum, National Gallery of Art in DC and Delaware Art Museum. It would be a long time before I received any responses.

A Proposition.

Excitedly I opened the letter from Mary Ann. She greeted me with "My Dearest Horace", and continued to explain that her Daddy had received the crate with the beautiful painting of her and her horse. He mailed the payment and told me not to hang it in any of the public areas of the house. He was not impressed with it and did not comment on it.

This was fine with me because it would hang in my bedroom opposite the Row House painting I already owned. "I simply adore the picture Horace", she wrote, "I must meet you alone in person to thank you in a very special way for such a wonderful picture".

It was already early September and I knew of her plans to depart for a long journey in Europe sometime in Autumn. In the letter she suggested we meet at the bridge about midday on the next Friday. "Daddy and Sally will be away, and we can enjoy the time alone, it is the perfect time and place for a romantic rendezvous.

Having never been propositioned by a beautiful lady I was tantalized and very excited. I hastily responded that I looked forward to our date and posted my response that same day.

Some Responses.

While waiting for the museums to answer my offer to loan my Pippin painting for exhibit I went against Jake's advice and contacted an appraiser I found online. In the meantime, my friend Matt who collects art and has a few pieces done by outside artists, suggested I contact a friend of his who specializes in this genre. This person could not offer much info about Pippin, but strongly suggested I visit a gallery here in Philadelphia. The owner Jon Harvard is considered an expert on Pippin.

The appraiser asked that I forward a copy of my report to him. He is internationally known for his knowledge of art as well as their value and the intricacies involved in the authentication process. Over the phone we shared stories of my old neighborhood where both my sister and his daughter had taken Irish dance lessons from the same instructor.

A discussion on my bridge painting bought his suggestion that I put the painting away for my grandchildren to discover, by then the scholar who has doubts would no longer be in the picture and the painting would be deemed authentic.

I found it an odd response, but Jake said it reinforced his experiences how some self-appointed experts could carry a lot of weight with their opinions no matter how off base they were. In other words, the appraiser was agreeing that my painting was the real deal but getting the scholar to agree would be difficult. He was taking a careful approach on protecting his reputation since he was not able to green light my painting. I accepted this and was not totally disappointed because it seemed to indicate that my research was working.

A Beautiful Day Begins.

Early Friday I packed my sketch materials, I learned always to have them along for whatever story might unfold. It was a glorious autumn day with lots of song birds sharing their melodies, the migration season looming. If I arrived early I would begin some sketches of the covered bridge. I remember the 3 paths that lead to and from the bridge, the mailbox to the side and the rolling tree lined hills in the background. I already had a spot picked out to set up my easel. It offered a vantage point where I could balance the square geometry of the bridge just to the side of a gentle rolling landscape.

It was close to 10 am when I rolled the bicycle to a stop just past the open mailbox and just left of the bridge. Late summer bees, chirping birds and scattering wildlife added to the beauty of the setting. Unfolding my small wooden easel, I went about composing a preliminary sketch with the far bank of the creek in front and to the right. The sun was still somewhat low in the sky to my left casting an attentive pattern of shadows across the entire scene.

Two hours passed quickly when suddenly I noticed movement far above on the path leading from the farm. There she was, "What a beautiful picture Mary Ann made" I exclaimed as she purposely approached carrying a large basket covered with a colorful quilt. She was dressed in a smart plunging blouse and a light blue skirt just brushing the top of her knees revealing the most beautiful and shapely legs I ever seen. No stockings with open tan sandals rounded off her outfit, just right for a picnic and perhaps something more.

I was glad I had taken time to look good, wearing a short sleeve pressed white shirt and a smart pair of khakis.

Mary Ann's bright wide smile was better than any words could speak in a welcoming greeting. She immediately took my hand with a firm grip, giving me a soft peck on my cheek and said, "Come with me".

More Responses.

Finally, a large envelope arrived from National Gallery of Art, Washington, DC. Inside was the report that I had mailed there and a handwritten note on their letterhead. It was from Nancy Anderson, the head curator of American Art at the museum. She thanked me for my offer to loan my Pippin, but the museum didn't have the room to exhibit all the pictures they have there. She recommended I contact the Brandywine River Art Museum.

Another letter arrived shortly afterwards, from Jessica Smith, Curator of American Art, Philadelphia Museum of Art. She thanked me for offering to lend my Pippin painting to the museum for exhibit but due to space constraints the museum would not be able to accept it at this time.

A third letter, this one from the American Folk Art Museum in NYC was a little more encouraging. Stacy Hollander, Chief Curator Director of Exhibitions wrote that she was grateful for me contacting them and offering my Pippin as a loan. She would pass along the info to an assistant and said I would be hearing from them. She also said that provenance would be of some significance in establishing the painting as the work of Pippin.

The only provenance I could offer at this time was the sale of the picture to me by Gino early February 2017 and his purchase of it from a local auction house a week before in a box lot. The picture was exhibited shortly after it was painted. The ghost marks where an exhibitor label was brushed with adhesive and the same size ghost of the placed label were evident on the back of the canvas board. It probably would be difficult to find exactly where it hung but the age marks indicated that it was exhibited shortly after it was painted probably 1940 or so. My guess was that it was a minor show or even one that was loaned to a store or library for a brief period.

Things Heat Up.

The temperature seemed to soar with her arrival as Mary Ann lead me off to a partially shaded and moss-covered area just below the bridge. It was close to the bubbling water of the stream and the melodic sounds added to the unique quality of the area. Sitting on the quilt we stared deeply into each other's eyes. Our lips joined, and her mouth opened widely.

I hardly remember saying much or for that matter eating anything. But the basket of food was empty, and a bottle of ale consumed. All I recalled was crazy fireworks going off in my head as we shared our most intimate selves repeatedly until we were spent.

Our naked bodies laid entwined and Mary Ann was sleeping with soft breaths emulating from her partially opened mouth. I refused to move so as not to disturb her peace and happiness. As I carefully slid off her I could not but help admire her beautiful body. I wondered how many times before she had made love like this? With such a protective daddy probably not so many times.

With Mary Ann soundly asleep and wrapped in the quilt, I dressed and returned to my easel to continue my sketching. Eventually I saw her stir from a distance as she gracefully dressed somewhat hidden using the quilt as a screen.

Next she was next to me laughing and crying at the same time as we held each other in a strong embrace.

The USPS.

I decided to send my report to a few more Museums including the MET and MOMA in NYC, the Smithsonian National Museum of African American History and Culture in DC and the Outsider Art Museum in Baltimore. Traveling to the post office to purchase stamps it occurred to me that it would be nice to use commemorative stamps for posting this group of requests.

At the counter I was amazed at the variety of stamps honoring Americans that were available for purchase. I ordered a sheet of stamps of a painting by Andrew Wyeth that I recognized from the many books I had read about his work. Thinking that is was N. C. Wyeth, Andrew's father, that helped in getting Pippin started in his climb to prominence, I wondered, why not a stamp honoring Horace Pippin. After all he was an American war hero, he was recognized as one of the most popular Folk Artist in America's modern times and my Covered Bridge painting would be a perfect subject with the open mail box right out front in the picture.

Inquiring about the commemorative stamp process the clerk said I could find all the info online. Returning home, I found the site for the Citizens' Stamp Advisory Committee and read all the requirements an art work to be considered for a stamp. I filled out an application, uploaded pictures and mailed a hard copy as well with high hopes of being considered.

Several weeks later I received a response; "Dear Mr. Hughes, thank you for your letter to the Citizens' Stamp Advisory Committee expressing support for the issuance of a commemorative stamp honoring Horace Pippin. I am pleased to inform you that this proposal will be submitted for review and consideration before the Citizens' Stamp Advisory Committee. The Advisory Committee is responsible for reviewing stamp proposals and making recommendations to the Postmaster General.

I thought to myself that if accepted as a stamp my covered bridge painting would have an amazing exposure to the public, much more so than being exhibited in a museum.

A Quiet Departure.

The silence that followed did not surprise me since it dawned on me that in the past 3 hours we hardly said more than a few words to each other. Yet at the same time I felt that I 've known this woman for ages.

Exhibiting a huge smile as she slowly released herself from our embrace Mary Ann said softly, "I must be getting back home, I want you to know that I never felt more complete than when I was with you".

This is when I noticed that the basket was repacked with the quilt folded on top. Still somewhat frozen in time I returned the smile and watched in wonder as she made her way climbing the hill to her home.

She turned once smiling and waving, little did I know this would be the last time I would see Mary Anne Pyle.

The sun now below the tree tops reminded me of the long pedal in front of me to return home. I arrived late that night already dark and collapsed into my bed to sleep the most peaceful night that I could remember.

In the Doldrums.

Almost 5 weeks passed with not much new research or museum exhibit responses. I was becoming a bit impatient and thought it was time to step up the inquires and get more people involved to authenticate my Pippin painting. I set aside an evening with a bottle of red wine to re-strategize my quest.

I reviewed all that I had compiled in the past 12-13 months and who I had contacted, spoke to or written and made notes of my recollections. It finally occurred to me that I had read several books on Pippin written by experts and had not sent any of these people a copy of my findings.

So once again, I tried to contact Judith Stein through the Art Critic, asking him to forward my report to her. I also sent copies to Jon Harvard at his gallery in Philadelphia and to Celeste-Marie Bernier author of Suffering and Sunset: World War I in the Art and Life of Horace Pippin. In this book Celeste writes about both Judith and Jon and some of the discussions they have concerning paintings done by Horace Pippin.

I have quick response from all three of these Pippin experts. Judith finds my report very interesting and convincing and mentions that she has forwarded it to a friend of hers who studies Pippin. Jon requests that I bring the painting into his gallery, so he can look at it first hand and Celeste thanks me for sharing my vitally important research with her.

I call Jon Harvard and make an appointment to meet him with my painting. We agree to meet the next week early on Tuesday morning.

Joy Turned to Sadness.

The rest of the Autumn and into the Winter of the new year was jam packed with engagements. There were shows in Chicago, San Francisco, Washington, DC, Baltimore and Boston. The overburdened schedule began to affect my health, first with bouts of exhaustion and then fits of depression. From lack of sleep I began to take medications that would turn out to do more harm than good.

On one late winter night as I looked out my window at the snowflakes lit up by the glowing gas lamp, I was reminded of a much younger boy, captivated by this mesmerizing scene. As I paused from my work at my easel I held up the canvas board and turned it toward the gas light to study this very emotional picture I was almost finished with.

I reflected on the joyful encounter with Mary Ann that glorious day at the covered bridge. For months afterwards, I was unsuccessful in contacting her. I knew she was in Europe with her sister and I was able to follow her itinerary through the society news in the local newspaper. Even though I mailed letters weekly I received no responses. Her daddy, leaving the homestead vacant, caught up with them shortly after their departure because of Mary Ann's sister Sally becoming ill. Unfortunately, he also came down with a serious malady and passed away before the end of the year. Sally recovered, and the two sisters settled in with the European relatives and never returned home.

The farm was donated to the Brandywine Conservancy who guaranteed it's upkept including the continued maintenance of the two bridges.

Interest in the Frame.

I set out early for a 10 o'clock meeting with Jon Harvard at the Philadelphia gallery which he has owned for decades. It was located on the upper floors of a mid-century hi-rise in center city. Departing the elevator, I entered through the glass doors and before reaching the receptionist a refined looking man came out from the far side and walking toward me ask if I was Tom Hughes. Greetings were exchanged, and I was invited to follow him into his office. On the coffee table was a giant manuscript type of a book that I inquired about. "That is by an outsider artist who will have a show here later this year". He asked if he could see the painting.

Taking the picture out of the cardboard box I was storing it in, I handed it to Jon. I was sitting on a couch across from him as he studied the picture carefully. I decided that it would be best for me to be quiet and not ask questions or offer any of my experiences over the past 14 months concerning the painting. After about 5 minutes he stood up and slowly walked over to the window and continued to look at the front and back of the piece for another 5 minutes, without saying a word.

Finally, Jon said, "I have handled over 200 purported Pippin paintings over the years of having a gallery and I cannot say that this is a forgery or a fake". It is a very interesting painting, not one of the Pippins that have been catalogued and it needs a good cleaning and minor repair where the paint is chipping. He had the copy of my report that I had sent him, and he opened it to the page where I discuss the size of the canvas board and how it was cut from a larger board. Going to his extensive library of books he took down a copy of Judith Stein's "I Tell My Heart, The Art of Horace Pippin" and opened it to the complimentary sized painting "The Art Critic" owned by the Philadelphia Art Museum. After doing the math he commented that it would be very interesting to have the two boards matched up at their cut edges. Jon asked if Judith Stein had seen the painting.

I told him that Judith had read the report, was piqued by it and forwarded to a friend. He said that he would talk to the scholar who was working at the Metropolitan Museum of Art of New York. At this I mentioned that if she would request to see the picture I would bring it to her.

Handing the picture back to me carefully Jon reminded me to take care of the conservation of the piece soon and make sure I have the right people do it. I thanked him for taking the time to examine the Pippin and insured him I would have it cleaned and treated. I put the painting back in the box, thanked him again and turned to leave when he stopped me. I was puzzled by his remark. "Tom, do you know what the most interesting thing I find about this painting". I say, no what is it? Then he surprises the heck out of me.

Jon says, "It is the frame", he says. I stop dead in my tracks and think, the frame that I was told would never be on a Pippin painting.

I ask him why the frame interests him so much? He goes to the bookcases again and opens another catalogue of Pippins work and point to two pictures done in 1939 and 1940 and says this frame is the same exact frame that was on these two Pippins that I handled here over the years.

I thanked him for this information thinking that it is great news. Returning to the van to drive home, I sighed a huge breath and thought to myself I am almost there with the authentication. I also make a mental note to talk to Russell later that day to discuss possible conservators.

Finishing the Story.

After reflecting on the gathering snow my attention returns to my brush and the portion of the sky which I was reworking by layering distinct colors of paint. The blue paint, remembering Mary Ann's skirt color that day, was all but gone now covered with a coat of yellow and a shimmer of gray on the top, creating the remembrance of a glorious sunset that receded to a more somber glow.

The covered bridge exhibited two dark gaping holes, at the road and underneath at the stream, representing unexplored avenues. The open mailbox with the red flag down signaled all the unanswered letters that I had sent in hopes of reconnecting with Mary Ann.

I changed the ground to freshly fallen snow because the seemingly eternal warmth of that day had faded away into a cold landscape. As I final statement I painted the double trunk tree with the other main stem freshly cut and now gone as a realization of Mary Ann being gone forever.

On the other hand the picture still had a positive quality. It was the strong overall presence of peace that still exuded from the picture that remained and reminded me of our forged love that was created on that day. This picture now, "Told My Heart as I Saw It".

News Moves Fast.

Only a few days later since meeting with Jon, the only Pippin expert I would see in person, a letter arrived from the MET.

Dear Mr. Hughes: Thank you for contacting the Metropolitan Museum of Art. President/CEO Daniel Weiss has forwarded your correspondence of February 10 concerning your work by Horace Pippin. As you may know Pippin is well represented in the Museum's collection and in our galleries. For that reason, we are not in need nor a position to borrow Mary Ann Pyle Bridge for the foreseeable future.
Even so, we appreciate your sharing the information about the painting with us. Best Wishes, Randall Griffey, Curator, Modern and Contemporary Art.

A week later the Smithsonian responded: Dear Mr. Hughes, Thank you for your letter of January 30, 2018 in which you proposed loaning a work from your collection by the artist Horace Pippin, which you call Mary Ann Pyle Bridge. The image(s) you included is (are) quite intriguing, and we would very much like to have a painting by Pippin. However, we rarely borrow works to be shown temporarily in our visual art gallery. We prefer, instead, to feature the works in our permanent collection. We appreciate your thinking of the National Museum of African American History and Culture and, should you ever plan to donate your Pippin, we would be very interested in considering such a gift. We congratulate on your detective work in connection with the painting and trust it will bring you great satisfaction.

With best regards, Jacquelyn D. Serwer, Chief Curator.

These two letters gave me satisfaction for two reasons. Finally, people at the top of the art world were recognizing my picture as a true Pippin and my hard and persistent work was finally paying off.

Not in the position to donate the painting at this time I set my next goal on having it conserved. I would call Russell to suggest a conservator for my Pippin picture.

A Brief Showing.

Prior to an upcoming show in which I would hang 3 of my paintings, I was asked at the last moment to hang 2 pictures for a 1 week show at the local Art Association annual fund raiser.

I only had 2 complete paintings in my studio, the Paul B. Dague Portrait and the Mary Ann Pyle Bridge picture. In haste I prepared two exhibitor labels with my name and title of each picture. Placing each upside down on the back of each painting I smeared them with paste, then turned them over and stuck them in another area. I waited until the ghost of the labels, now rectangular outlines of paste to dry.

Early that evening I took the 2 paintings to the Art Association and left them for the show. Since I was traveling to Baltimore for a week I would not be able to attend.

Upon returning from my trip I learned that the Sheriff himself had bought his portrait and that the Bridge did not sell. It would be another week or so before I could find the time to pick it up and bring it back home.

Simon Parkes.

Wanting to share my experience of the meeting with Jon Harvard with someone, I met Russell for breakfast. I thought he would be able to suggest a conservator for my Pippin picture.

He was excited to hear my news and asked what I would do with the painting now that it was authenticated. Responding I said, "I am sticking to my original 2-year plan which was to show it was done by Pippin, loan it for exhibition somewhere and write a book. It would be about my experiences of finding the painting and the work involved in having it deemed the real thing coupled with a historic fictional novel of Pippin's life. In my extensive research of Pippin, I found some parallels to things I experienced growing up.

Russell strongly suggested that I take my painting to Simon Parkes in NYC. He had a painting treated by him years ago and even though it was expensive he was very pleased with the results. Simon Parkes had a very good reputation and was the go to person for Sotheby's Auction House when it needed conservation work done.

Later that night I sent an email to Simon along with a copy of my report which by now had many photos of the picture. A few days later a response came saying yes, he would do the cleaning and repair the area where a couple of small chips of paint were missing. The price would be $1600.

Russell had mentioned that it would not be inexpensive, but the work would be done carefully and correctly. I took my Pippin to NYC the next day and left it for conservation.

Pippin Peppers.

On my return from Baltimore I was sure to pick up the Bridge Painting. Taking it back home I was pleased that it did not sell. That night in my studio I changed my mind about hanging it and instead found a cozy spot in the closet opposite my dresser. It fit nicely on the top shelf and would remain there for a very long time.

Coming to the kitchen the next morning I remembered the bag of peppers that I had bought back from Baltimore. A cousin there grew them on his farm and made a pepper sauce that was very popular in his small restaurant. I found them very tasty, spicy and liked their beautiful purple color. Now I had a couple dozen or so to enjoy and perhaps save and dry the seeds for next year's garden. I would share them with Mr. Weaver who also kept a garden and was very good at saving seeds. So good that the pepper was picked up by a local seed company who named them the Pippin Pepper. Today they are still available from the Baker Creek Seed Company in Lancaster, PA.

Sotheby's Steps In.

I picked up my Pippin painting from Simon Parkes three weeks later and was very pleased with the conservation. The painting never having been cleaned before was given a very gentle wash that revealed the various muted colors that Pippin had used. The green color was much more evident, the orange hue effect of the sky more brilliant and the snow much less yellow.

The most amazing part of the conservation was the stabilizing done where the paint had been chipping a little and the rebuilding of material that matched exactly the brush strokes and color of the surrounding area. It was the best investment I could have made to preserve my painting.

Remembering that my Pippin had not been insured, I sent a copy of my report along with before and after pictures of the conservation work to Sotheby's Auction to request an estimate if it were to be offered for sale. A reply comes very quickly.

Resting Places.

With the Mary Ann Pyle Bridge picture in an appropriate resting place, I continue my demanding schedule to produce more paintings for the increasing number of shows, exhibits and commissions that continue to come.

I find myself fighting exhaustion and depression, losing contact with friends and taking medications that are supposed to help me but only make me worse.

On a local park bench one day in late Autumn, I am bundled up to be warm against a strong and chilly wind. I am at complete rest as I look out over the park green with trees that have already turned their leaves a sharp tan color. I decide I will paint this scene and in the last version I am resting on the bench which is colored a bright red.

I am alone except for a bright white squirrel gathering nuts for winter. I find this scene very peaceful and in it a life to continue after the cold harsh winter. However, I never see the coming Spring because I pass away before it rises. I lived a very fulfilling life and was blessed to be able to tell my stories through my paintings.

Next Up?

Sotheby's wishes to sell my Pippin as indicated in their response. *"Dear Tom, thank you for taking the time to speak with me yesterday and for providing additional information on your wonderful Horace Pippin. It is an excellent example of this rare artist's work and we would be very pleased to work with you on its sale. We've been able to review the images and information on the work and would recommend presenting this painting at auction with a pre-sale estimate of $60,000-80,000. We are confident that offering your Pippin at this level will indicate the importance of the work while simultaneously creating enthusiastic bidding in the salesroom. We had great success offering another work by the artist in our most recent American Art sale and thus now have the most up-to-date information on the collectors most actively seeking examples of his work. We believe we are well-positioned to achieve a similarly competitive result on your behalf. Please let me know if you would like to discuss our recommendations for your Pippin in further detail and I'd be happy to give you a call. Thank you again for contacting us about this wonderful work. Sincerely yours, Elizabeth Pisano."*

I am very happy with the estimate they supply, and I use it to get a price on insuring my picture. I find an affordable premium; however, the picture must go to a climate controlled, fire proof and secure location. The only place I can come up with seems to be the Auction House. I plan a visit to talk to them and show them my painting.

At this point I am still waiting to hear from the USPS review committee to see if the picture will become a commemorative stamp. Can I find a museum that will exhibit my Pippin for a brief period?

My visit to Sotheby's proves to be fruitful, if I leave the painting there it would be covered by their insurance. I receive a property receipt form them and leave the painting in their hands. Later I decide to have it listed for auction in their catalogue the following Spring.

Time will tell what happens to the painting from there on. For me it has offered one of the most exciting journeys I have experienced. I feel enriched to have found Horace Pippin.

The End.

APPENDIX

Mary Ann Pyle Bridge

Laurels Preserve
Brandywine Conservancy

Oil painting on canvas board

H. Pippin

This picture was purchased at a flea market in Adamstown, PA on a Sunday morning in February 2017, from a dealer who bought it the previous week at a local auction in a box lot.

The picture was signed H Pippin. Research was begun to learn more about Horace Pippin, his life, his art work and this painting which is referenced by me as the Mary Ann Pyle Bridge (reason to follow).

The first task was to take the painting to the Rago Auction house in Lambertville NJ to show it to Tom Martin (this on advice from an antique dealer friend). Mr. Martin and an appraiser colleague mentioned that the painting was the correct age and style of Horace Pippin's art and suggested that research begin at the Free Library of Philadelphia. I was told that valuable resource information about Horace Pippin could be found there.

At the Library was a book titled, "I Tell My Heart The Art of Horace Pippin" written by Judith E. Stein who is an expert on Pippin and his work. This book has been very helpful in identifying important characteristics of Horace Pippin's art.

On the next page is a photo of both the front and back of the Mary Ann Pyle Bridge Painting with reference letters A, B…….H, I, which help in cross referencing the important points of this report.

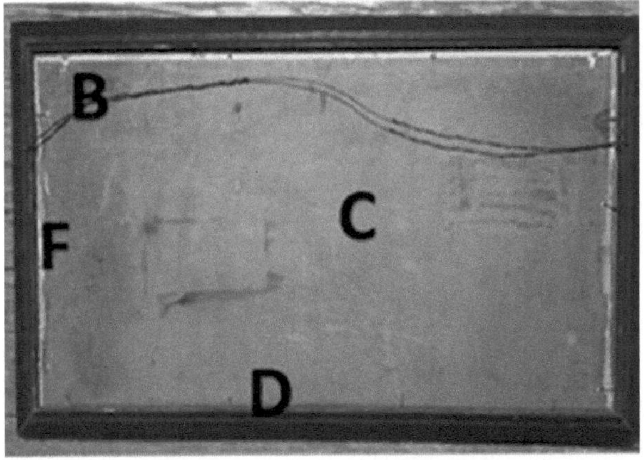

A

The Mary Ann Pyle Bridge painting is of the style used by Horace Pippin in his paintings. This style includes flat forms, unusual color combinations and the lack of perspective. Pippin would usually apply house paint in thick short strokes often using grays, black, greens and brown and occasionally a splash of red. These characteristics are evident in the Mary Ann Bridge painting.

B

The Mary Ann Pyle Bridge painting is on a canvas board which was a common material used by Horace Pippin. The board measures 24"x14 1/2" and has a supplier stamp on the back that reads "A & B Smith Company, Pittsburg 30 PA."

I contacted the company which is still in business today and received the following email from them.

"Mr. Hughes,
A&B Smith [Almart] has been in business since 1914 so we very well could have supplied stores in West Chester PA in the 30's and 40's. We have no records dating back that far, but it's good to know our products are withstanding the test of time. Thank you for contacting us.
Regards,
Marty Smith"

The address on the stamp shows a postal district (30) which was used during Horace Pippin's time, instead of zip codes which are common today, giving some idea as to the age of the board.

C

Two other properties of the board are important to note.
First there is an indication of an exhibitor's label that was once attached to the board. The photo of the back of the board on page 4 shows a glue ghost around a placed label just left of the board center, the label was then turned over and
pasted down just right of the board center.
Pippin was known to have exhibited his work in such shows as the Chester County Art Association (CCAS) show and the West Chester Community Center show as noted in Judith Stein's book. (1)

D

Secondly, the Mary Ann Pyle bridge board is cut neatly along one of the 24" edges. (see below)

It was common for Pippin to cut canvas boards for different paintings as mentioned by Judith Stein, "Pippin cut down a canvas panel to a smaller size to use for Chester County Art Critic (1940)". (2)
It is interesting to note that the height of the Art Critic painting is 21 1/2", which is the supplement (considering a standard 36" tall standard size board) to the 14 1/2" height of the Mary Ann Pyle bridge painting. (see diagram following).

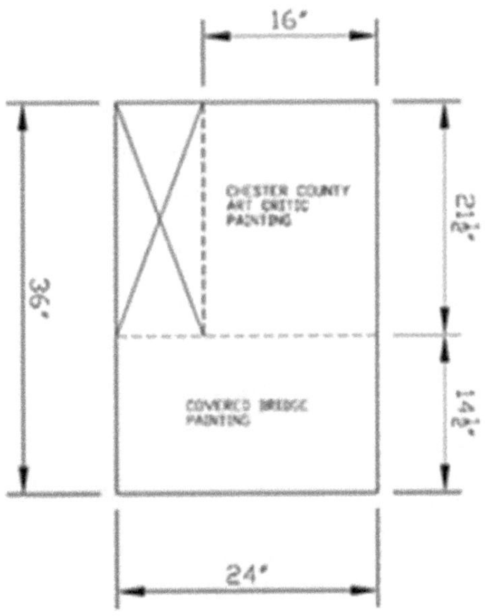

Common canvas panel size 24 x 36 inches

E

The subject of the painting was found by searching the internet for maps that show covered bridges in Chester County PA., an area where Pippin painted. An aerial view of one such map indicates a road pattern that seems to match the geometry of the roads (paths) depicted in the painting. A walk along such paths in the Laurals Preserve of the Brandywine Conservancy will bring oneself to two bridges known as the Speakman #1 & #2 covered bridges. One of these bridges formally known as the Mary Ann Pyle Bridge is the bridge in the painting.
See the following diagram that matches a photo of the actual bridge which was built in 1865 with the bridge depicted in the painting.

The remaining cross references F, G, H & I pertain to the highlighting of characteristics of the Mary Ann Pyle bridge that match aspects of technique appearing in many of Horace Pippin's paintings.

F

Pippin would layer many colors to achieve different effects

Paul B. Dague, Deputy Sheriff of Chester County

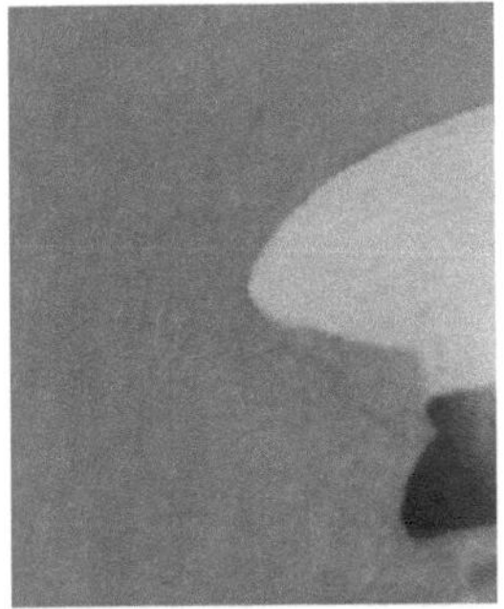

Saturday Night Bath

Mary Ann Pyle Bridge

This layering effect is also evident on the edges and rear of the canvas board where the distinct colors bled over. As Judith Stein mentions about "The Getaway" painting (1939). (5)

"Also evident on the reverse (rear or back of the support) are brighter blue colors in the sky than are now visible on the front and red under layers to what are yellow-gray clouds".

The same condition occurs on the rear of the board in the Mary Ann Pyle Bridge Painting where the sky is on the front.

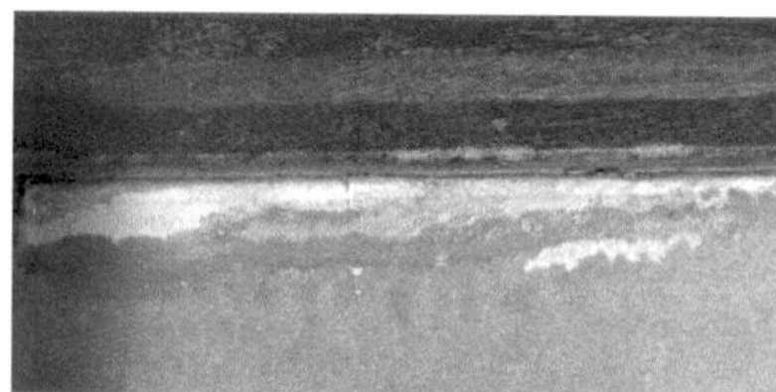

G

Horace Pippin often added a splash of red to his scenes as noted by Jen Bryant in her book, " A Splash of Red". "Every day, and late into the night, Horace worked on his painting. He used gray, black, and white, the somber colors of war. Here and there, he added a splash of red." (6) page 25

A splash of red also occurs in the Mary Ann Pyle Bridge painting as the flag on the mailbox. (see below)

H

Colors in Horace Pippin's work. Noted by Judith Stein, "In Pippin's early works, the palette tends towards simple, often muted color combinations. Dorothy C. Miller quotes Pippin: "How I Paint; The colors are simple such as brown, amber, yellow, black, white and green". (7) page 174

These colors are present in the Mary Ann Pyle Bridge painting as shown in a portion of the painting shown here.

I

In her book "I Tell My Heart The Art of Horace Pippin", Judith Stein notes the following.

"The majority of Pippin's paintings are signed, invariably in the lower right corner. Generally, the signatures are in the form "H. PiPPiN" with the letters in a combination of upper and lower cases." (7) page 176

The signature in the Mary Ann Pyle Bridge painting is shown here.

Horace Pippin's signature

The size of the letters used for the signature in the Mary Ann Pyle Bridge painting is consistent with the size of the letters in most of Pippin's works.

I examined many sizes of paintings done by Pippin, from 8 x 10 inches 16 x 21 1/2 inches, in most cases the signature letters are 1/2 inch in height regardless of the canvas size.

The size of the letters used for the signature in the Mary Ann Pyle Bridge painting are 1/2 inch in height.

Bibliography

"I Tell My Heart The Art of Horace Pippin"
written by Judith E. Stein

(1) page(s) 8, 10
(2) page(s) 172, 103
(3) page 101
(4) page 149
(5) page 182
(7) page 174
(8) page 176

" A Splash of Red"
written by Jen Bryant

(6) page 25